What Are You Going to Do with Your Life?

BOOKS BY EDWIN H. FRIEDMAN

Generation to Generation
Friedman's Fables
The Myth of the Shiksa and Other Essays
A Failure of Nerve: Leadership in the Age of the Quick Fix

WHAT
ARE YOU
GOING TO DO
with
YOUR LIFE?

UNPUBLISHED WRITINGS AND DIARIES

EDWIN H. FRIEDMAN

Seabury Books
New York

Library of Congress Cataloging-in-Publication Data
Friedman, Edwin H.
What are you going to do with your life? : unpublished essays and diaries / Edwin Friedman.
    p.   cm.
Includes bibliographical references.
ISBN 978-1-59627-114-2 (pbk.)
1. Friedman, Edwin H. 2. Friedman, Edwin H.—Diaries. 3. Rabbis—United States—Diaries. 4. Jewish sermons, American. 5. Life-cycle, Human—Religious aspects—Judaism. 6. Self-actualization (Psychology)—Religious aspects—Judaism. I. Title.
BM755.F727A5 2009
296.8'341092—dc22
                          2008055495

Cover design by Stefan Killen
Interior design by Vicki K. Black

Printed in the United States of America.

Seabury Books
445 Fifth Avenue
New York, New York 10016
Seabury Books is an imprint of Church Publishing Incorporated
www.churchpublishing.com

5　4　3　2　1

Table of Contents

Part Three
ACCEPTING MORTALITY

About Edwin H. Friedman

Born and raised in New York City, Edwin H. Friedman (1932–1996) was an ordained rabbi and practicing family therapist. Reared on Manhattan's Upper West Side, he graduated from Bucknell University and earned a doctorate of divinity at Hebrew Union College, where he was ordained in 1959.

Rabbi Friedman was intimately involved in politics, religion, and psychotherapy in the Washington, D.C., metropolitan area for nearly forty years. He was rabbi at Temple Shalom in Chevy Chase, Maryland, when he joined the Johnson White House as a community relations specialist, and in 1964 he became the founding rabbi of the Bethesda Jewish Congregation.

His groundbreaking *Generation to Generation,* published in 1985, applies Bowen family systems theory to religious and other institutions. Praised by leaders of all faiths, it has become a handbook for understanding the connection between emotional process at home and at work in religious, educational, therapeutic, and business systems and is now required reading in many universities and seminaries throughout the United States. *Friedman's Fables,* published in 1990, uses the ancient art form of the fable to offer fresh perspectives on human foibles, based on the author's insights into emotional process, while the many-faceted essays collected in *The Myth of the Shiksa* are popular teaching materials in courses and at workshops and conferences. Theories which Friedman developed in this earlier work, moreover, he extended to the concepts of leadership in *A Failure of Nerve: Leadership in the Age of the Quick Fix,* published after his death.

Friedman was in great demand as a consultant and public speaker, presenting workshops and lectures in almost every state and in many countries before a wide variety of professional and lay audiences. During the last ten years of his life, he led workshops for groups of Episcopal bishops, Trappist abbots and abbesses, members of Congress, state governors and their staffs, the General Staff of the United States Army in Europe, and the executive committee of the Chief of Naval Operations. His Center for Family Process in Bethesda trained people from the medical and psychotherapy professions as well as government and business leaders.

Editors' Foreword

In the early days of 2007, Ed Friedman's daughter, Shira Friedman Bogart, found herself face-to-face with her father's past—an eight-foot file cabinet filled with diaries, sermons, and unpublished manuscripts. Although Shira and her brother had published several books since their father's death, Shira was overwhelmed and immobilized with the volume of work until her brother, Ari Friedman, remarked, "Why don't we just publish them?"

So in the late summer of 2007, Ari and Shira invited two people who were instrumental in the posthumous publication of their father's works, *A Failure of Nerve* and *The Myth of the Shiksa,* to go through his remaining manuscripts. Were they important enough to salvage from drawers, boxes, and files for future publication? Peggy Treadwell and Cynthia Shattuck spent several days at the family home in Bethesda reading essays, sermons, and journals that dated all the way back to a diary Ed Friedman kept during his first year of rabbinical studies, and as far forward as a visit he records to a family cemetery not long after his own brush with mortality in the form of heart surgery. As a family therapist, rabbi, and orator, Ed Friedman spent a lifetime helping people navigate the cycles of life and the challenges they bring. So it was no surprise that the major themes which emerged clustered around "rites of passage," specifically the transitions of high school and college years, the discovery of vocation, the occasions of weddings and funerals, the onset of old age, and the acceptance of mortality. To sum up this collection of writings and diaries, it seemed only fitting to choose a working title from one of the baccalaureate addresses, "What Are You Going to Do with Your Life?"

We decided to group these pieces according to the human life cycle, from youth to old age. The first section, "Starting Out," is directly addressed to youth—it begins with two baccalaureate talks given at local Washington, D.C., high schools and a talk to the youth of his congregation in the greater Washington area. The longest piece, "A Reason for Living," is made up of selections from a diary chronicling Ed's first year of rabbinical school. He describes his deep connection with his chosen vocation, but also experiences tremendous conflict between a passion for study and self-improvement and his desire for human love and commitment. This section ends with three wedding sermons that were given at Temple Shalom and the Bethesda Jewish Congregation, where he was the founding rabbi.

We learn that the roots of Ed's attraction to the rabbinate lay further back than Bucknell University, from which he had graduated the spring before. Because he spent the first sixteen years of his life rooming with his grandmother, Judaism had found a secret passage to his core. Ed also found himself one of the few Jews in college at Bucknell University. He did not incur any hatred or prejudice, just a dearth of knowledge on the subject. He enjoyed telling stories to the other students and by the time graduation arrived, Judaism was the vehicle that allowed him to pursue his path. A few days before Ed's graduation, on the night before his twenty-second birthday, his own father succumbed to a battle with hypertension. Ed left for Hebrew Union College soon after, filled with confusion and loss. While Bucknell had started his flirtation with wisdom, studying the Talmud made it an obsession. In just his first year of seminary, Ed's questions about love, life, and the universe changed daily. And with each year, his unconventional thoughts grew stronger. He was trouble. He doubted everything and everyone.

He and his best friend decided to take a year off and go to Israel; it was Ed's recollection that the school was relieved to be rid of them for a year. However, the experience only fueled his unruliness. After a year of speaking fluent Hebrew, shoveling eggplants on a *kibbutz,* and following the path of the Torah both in mind and body, he returned more contentious than before. Ed had seen the motherland and believed there was little left to teach him.

Ordained in 1959, he was pushed out of his first congregation, Temple Shalom in Chevy Chase, Maryland, after less than five years. The triangles of sabotage and insecurity that had led to his demise, he learned, were inherent to his leadership role. Ed would later teach others how to navigate through their own triangles. After a stint as a community relations specialist in the Lyndon Johnson White House, Ed returned to the rabbinate in 1964 to form his own flock as the founding rabbi of the Bethesda Jewish Congregation. Reconstructionist Judaism, the youngest and least traditional branch of Judaism, and the field of family therapy had both emerged, and Ed believed these movements shared his pioneering spirit. Little did he know that his "mad dog persistence" would uniquely merge the two.

These influences come together in Part Two, "The Challenges of Maturity," and it is where the first piece, "The Joy of Discovery," begins. This sermon for Columbus Day and the beginning of the Jewish New Year states for the first time the ideas that we see many years later in his opening chapter of *A Failure of Nerve* on the discoveries of the earliest explorers. He writes here, "As with Columbus, it is a choice of living forever in a world that is old or trying to discover one that is new. And as with the Torah, it is a choice of being satisfied with interpretations of an age gone by, or exploring the old for revelations that are new."

The next two essays build on the insights of the family therapy movement: "Systems and Ceremonies: A Family View of Rites of Passage" and "Rites of Passage: When the Parents Are No Longer Partners." Both explore family dynamics at significant turning points—not only the rites of pubescence, marriage, and death, but also transitional events that are now all too common—the uprooting caused by divorce, geographical mobility, and retirement. The section concludes with two very different pieces, both of which emerge out of his preaching (which he preferred to call teaching) in the synagogue. The first is a New Year's meditation on the corruptions of knowledge and power in modern life, particularly the human vanity and hubris let loose by atomic testing and the arms race, and the second a gently mocking dialogue with God on human maturity and responsibility.

In the decade that followed, Ed experienced the birth of both his children, some intense family of origin work revolving around his mother's seventieth birthday, and finally her painful decline and eventual death. The stress and sabotage he had experienced in his work as both rabbi and therapist also began to take its toll throughout the 1970s. As sabotage usually goes, it gnaws at its victims so slowly that the damage is often undetectable until recovery is nearly impossible. This is what happened to Ed's body. His mind was so deep in thought that it did not occur to him and his kosher heart that his inability to walk half a block without physical exhaustion was probably a bad sign. A trip to the cardiologist in the fall of 1980 uncovered heart problems, and a series of tests confirmed the suspicions. At the age of forty-eight, Ed had major arterial blockage and required immediate quadruple bypass surgery.

But how was he going to fit it in? There were the lectures and the clients and the travels. It was a true epiphany when he realized he could not make an impact on society if he were dead. At the time, he was told the surgery would add another ten years to his life. The race was on. His time now had an end. And he had things to do. Paradigms to shift. Worlds to move. Although Ed had already stirred up trouble in many disciplines, it was his finite existence that pushed him every day.

The book's final section, "Accepting Mortality," contains a great deal of Ed's meditations on family history and mortality, some the result of his medical condition. It begins with selections from the diary he kept during his diagnosis, surgery, and recovery. Although terrified and in denial at first, Ed also took it as a great opportunity. In *A Failure of Nerve,* he talked about the ways this process of surgery and recovery gave him the opportunity to work on himself and his family relationships. "How to Get Your Parent into a Nursing Home" and "Old Age: Condition or Diagnosis?" show how he put his theories into practice while navigating his mother's aging and decline. He chronicles how he manages his own emotions and avoids sabotage in the face of others' illness and anxiety. In addition, we see his personal work traversing the triangles that exist in any family system.

The final piece, "Between Two Cemeteries," records a visit to family graves some time after his bypass surgery and recovery. The essay is full of memories about childhood family outings, his grand-parents' graves located "somewhere between old neighborhoods of long-forgotten dates and friends, surrounded by a baseball stadium built for a team not then in existence and the grounds of the 1964 World's Fair." As he writes about the old metal relics of the fair-ground, which is now only an abandoned place for children to play, we see that we have come full circle from over twenty years before. In the much earlier piece "Change Too Must Change" in Part One, Ed speaks to the graduating seniors of Albert Einstein High about the optimism and excitement of the World's Fair that had opened in New York less than two months before, in April 1964—and which he calls "the nearest thing to a time machine that a human being can encounter."

This book has something for everyone. Passages that do not seem relevant now may, in time, become invaluable beacons of in-spiration inviting us to change. It not only outlines the cycles of life, it also takes the reader on a voyage through a great mind's life of self-discovery. As we uncover Ed Friedman's strengths and vul-nerabilities, we are reminded of our own mortality. And all that can be accomplished in a lifetime.

SHIRA FRIEDMAN BOGART
MARGARET M. (PEGGY) TREADWELL
CYNTHIA SHATTUCK
editors

Part One

STARTING OUT

What Are You Going to Do with Your Life?

Baccalaureate address given at Montgomery Blair High School, June 19, 1960

It is the custom of rabbis when they are to preach a sermon to base that sermon on a phrase or idea from the portion of the five books of Moses that is scheduled for that sabbath. The portion scheduled for this past week was from the book of Numbers and it had to do, interestingly enough, with a spy story. It is all about the twelve spies that Moses sends out to bring back information about the promised land—you will notice, by the way, that careful record is made as to who was responsible for the mission. Now when these spies return, all except two spread a report that the people they saw in Canaan looked to them like giants. And, they continued, "We appeared in their eyes as grasshoppers."

But this is a most extraordinary statement, "We appeared in their eyes as grasshoppers." For how can any of us know how we appear in the eyes of another? We can't. It is just such a question that some rabbis, many centuries ago, asked about this same biblical statement. "How do you know how you appeared in their eyes?" asked the rabbis. "Maybe," they went on, "you appeared in their eyes as giants." It is a similar question that I would like to ask you this evening: namely, do you see yourself as the reflection of how you think you appear in the eyes of others? For, as you can see from the very asking of the question posed by these rabbis, it can be very misleading to assume because what you see outside of yourself appears large, that you therefore are small.

Moreover, even if we reverse the situation, we still find a similar danger. That is, it would be just as faulty to assume that you are big if everything outside of yourself appeared in your eyes as small. In other words, if all appear to you as grasshoppers then you are a giant. Thus not only may you *not* be a grasshopper when others appear to you as giants, but even if others come to you and tell you that you are a grasshopper, this may not be the case. For when we human beings seek to find our value, our worth, our dignity, we must not be guided by what appears outside of us nor even by what speaks to us from the outside. Rather we must be guided by what appears to us from inside, by what speaks to us from the inside.

For you see, dignity is very important to a human being—it is in fact what makes you human and what differentiates you from other forms of life. A human being is the only form of life that truly senses shame, and is not shame by its very nature a loss of dignity? You can have a sense of shame only if you have a sense of dignity to lose. And this sense of dignity comes not from without, but from within. You will remember the story in Genesis about Adam and Eve. Sometimes this tale is referred to as the fall of Adam—it is much less the story of his fall than of his rise, which is described here. For is this not a tale of how the first human beings felt for the first time ashamed—felt a loss of dignity? The inference then is that for the first time, human beings felt that they had dignity to lose. And how did they learn that they had dignity? Did someone tell them? Did they see something? The answer to both questions is no! Their sense of dignity did not come from without, either by comparison to the slimy snake or even by word from the great God. It came from within, after they had tasted of the fruit of knowledge.

All of you have been tasting of—indeed, feasting on—the fruit of knowledge for quite some time now. And all of you will continue to eat of it throughout your lives. Some of you will favor the more academic variety and some of you will find that the flavor of practical experience better suits your taste. But all of you will continue to learn and all of you will continue to experience. And as you do, your sense of dignity should increase.

But even as this process goes on, you are going to come into contact with gigantic forces telling you that you have no more dignity than a grasshopper. And these forces will appear to you as so gigantic that you may be misled into thinking that you are smaller than you are. What are these forces which threaten your dignity and how can you cope with them? Upon what can you rely to gain the self-confidence, the inner security that will preserve your dignity in the face of these giants?

These gigantic forces which threaten the dignity of the human being today are massive. They may be divided into two categories, for they operate in two different ways. The first category is that of armed might. You belong to the first generation in the history of humankind that will grow up in an age when the world can go up in smoke, when the technology of war has become so intricate that human beings have been robbed of their responsibility to defend themselves and of their responsibility or even ability to prevent or initiate hostilities. Such a gigantic force is almost mystical. It tells us we are slaves to what we cannot see—an atom. It is a case of the powerless giant and the almighty grasshopper.

In such a time it is all too easy to say that the machinery of government is as intricate as the machinery of war. "I can have no say in the matter. What do I matter? There is no use in even thinking about it." And the next step down the ladder of dignity leads to a retreat into "Live for today, for tomorrow I may die." It leads you to escape from the worries of how you might die and even into the worries of how you might live. But you should be concerned with how you are going to die because it is part and parcel of how you are going to live.

The second group of forces is more subtle. These too seek obliteration of your dignity. They too are massive. They may not take away your lives, but they will take away your dignity and make your lives worthless. Among these are automation, the huge organizational complexes that govern your job, your education, your religion, your neighborhood, and even the way that you play, and the mass media of communication telling you what you should buy, what you should enjoy, and even what is happening to you. They seek to influence you and overpower you—and not even you as individuals, but as part of the mass.

In such a time, it is all too easy to begin to believe that you are really nothing more than a grasshopper, one of a swarm of grasshoppers blown hither and thither by the winds of public opinion, moving this way or that way simply because the swarm is moving this way or that way. Worst of all, you are not even able to tell which way the swarm is moving because there are too many in the swarm and the swarm itself is a giant.

And if we remember that knowledge is essential to human dignity, then certainly of first importance is where you are going, what are your goals—what, to coin a phrase, are you going to do with your life? That question which appears in your programs as the title of this talk was worded very carefully. It does not ask, "What are you going to do when you grow up?" or "What will you do when you go out into the world?" or "What are you going to do in life?" It asks, "What are you going to do *with* your life?" The emphasis is on the word "with." For your life belongs to you. There is a tremendously important assumption underlying that title, one that stands up to all the forces that will negate your sense of dignity. It is the assumption that you can have something to do with your life, that you can influence it, that you do not have to be what the world is forcing you to be.

Furthermore, it is not a question that asks you to answer; rather, it is a question that asks you to question. In the words of a rabbi-teacher of mine, addressed also to a graduating class, if you do not have answers, do not feel too badly. But if you do not have questions, you had better feel your pulse.

Now if I do not expect that any of you have ready answers for the problem of how to preserve your own personal dignity in the face of these forces, neither can I be expected to have ready answers myself. There are no ready answers. Each one of us must find our dignity in our own way. For dignity is partially the result of the uniqueness of one's own individual personality. I can give you no individual answers but I may be able to give you an approach, a guide, or plan for living, that will at least ensure that you will be conscious of your dignity.

What then would be the nature of such an approach; what would be its characteristics? First at all, it would be an approach to life that seeks earnestly and honestly what life has to offer. It would be an approach that would never be afraid to question what has come down from the past, and would realize that the answers given in the past were to questions raised in the past. But today new questions have arisen and the answers may not be the same.

For no matter how lucrative your job, how conservative your politics, how secluded your home, how liberal your politics, how segregated your race, how large your donations to charity, how often you go to church—these answers that might still satisfy the old questions will not take the place of your concern for what your government is going to do with your life or your concern for what you are going to do with your life.

It is an approach to the problems of life which is, above all, concerned with meeting these problems, accepting their challenges, never seeking refuge from them. An approach, in short, which seeks those answers that will enable us to grant ultimate respect to the human personality, and this no matter what the cost to our traditional beliefs and attitudes. For truth is the fluid in the spinal column of life. As long as it flows through our experience, our lives are supple and we can adjust to the quick and the uncertain. When it dries up, our lives lose the capacity to adapt, become rigid and inflexible, human being appears out of proportion, and the dignity of a human being is bent out of shape.

The second aspect of the approach is perhaps even more important. It requires that you understand what is meant by the dignity of a human being. Because the question "What are you going to do with your life?" was not meant to be restricted to what are you going to do for a living. It's an odd expression, isn't it?—"do for a living." We human beings seem to define ourselves according to our professions rather than according to our natures. As Eric Fromm, the well-known psychiatrist, has pointed out, if you could ask a chair what it was and it could talk, it would undoubtedly tell you, "a chair"; a table, and it would tell you, "a table." But ask people what they are and they will tell you a doctor, a lawyer, a businessman, a government worker, a housewife, a secretary. Rarely will one think of oneself first of all as a person, much more rarely as a human being.

To take the raw materials of which you are made, your special qualities, your interests, your abilities, and your talents, and pour them into a mold made by the demands of society is to show the ultimate contempt for the individuality out of which springs your dignity. True respect for your own dignity can only come when you find that role in society which most integrates the uniqueness of your personality, and which will enable you to be most productive in contributing to that society.

Finally, it is an approach characterized by a genuine love for the reality of experience, for the desire to encounter experience for its own sake. By the realization that experience is life itself and we were made to live it. Experience is the matrix through which the dignity, the individuality, of the human being receives its *raison d'être*. The dignity, the sacredness of human beings obtains its value, is enhanced, not by the getting of experience, but by the living of it. We are not machines to be broken in that we might work better! That we can do a better job after experience no one can deny. But if we look upon experience as merely something practical, as a breaking-in process, then we have lost the value of life.

Like Moses, you are preparing to enter a new land, to make your conquests there. Like Moses you have heard reports that there are massive giants there that threaten, swiftly or slowly, to crush from you your life and dignity. But you have not been told that in the face of such giants you are grasshoppers. For in the final analysis, it is not what society expects of you that should shape your life and determine your dignity, or lack of it, but rather what you expect of yourself that should shape and dignify you, shape and grant dignity to your society.

Change Too Must Change

Baccalaureate address given at Albert Einstein High School,
June 14, 1964

Next summer I imagine many of you would like to visit the World's Fair. They are always such exciting and attractive adventures, these opportunities to explore time and see a profile of change, to visit the future, as it were. A World's Fair, I think, is the nearest thing to a time machine that a human being can encounter. Thus it is not surprising that at each of these fairs, some kind of capsule containing evidence of the present is entombed for some lucky archeologist to find several centuries hence, and compare how his world has changed from ours.

At the 1939 fair in New York, Albert Einstein was asked, among others, to place some message in that time capsule. Part of his brief message of twenty-five years ago to the people of the future read as follows:

> Our time is rich in inventive minds, the inventions of which could facilitate our lives considerably. We utilize power in order to relieve humanity from all tiring, muscular work. We have learned to fly, and to send news without any difficulty over the entire world....
>
> However the production and distribution of commodities is unorganized so that everybody must live in fear of

the economic cycle. Furthermore, people living in different countries kill each other at irregular time intervals, so that for this reason anyone who thinks about the future must live in fear and terror. . . .

I trust that posterity will read these statements with a feeling of proud and justified superiority.

Alas, as far as we are part of that posterity to which Einstein was speaking, we have no justification for feeling proud or superior. To think of that future is still terrifying, and for much the same reasons that existed a quarter-century ago. In this respect there has been little change. If anything has changed, it seems to be not the reasons for fearing the future but rather the swiftness and the intensity with which those reasons come upon us.

It is a truism to say that the only permanent thing in the world is change. But, of course, if everything changes, then change too must change. And it is—changing for the faster. Change seems to me to be changing in the ratio of a geometric progression, so that each generation finds itself further removed from its predecessor. The ideas, the tastes, the art of the next generation are always a little farther out; the gap between children and their parents always a little wider than it had been for parents and their parents. And one of the most disrupting aspects of all this is that for you who are growing up, the conventional bridges that have traditionally spanned the generations—country, religion, race—are becoming inadequate because things become old-fashioned before they have been tried. There is little, it would appear, that is stable or permanent, little that can be relied upon to remain the same, to serve as a fixed star and help us chart the course of our future lives.

I grew up during World War II, so I was taught to hate the Germans, to despise the Japanese, and to dislike the Italians. The Chinese were good guys and so were the Turks and the Russians. For my parents who had grown up during World War I, it was quite disconcerting. They had been taught to hate the Turks, and to consider the Japanese and Italians as friends, and they had already been indoctrinated with fear of the new, young Communist Russia. Well, in a way, they'll get along better with my children than I will, for today once more the Japanese and the Italians are our friends and the Russians are again the bad guys.

When I was growing up, Negroes were porters on trains, now and then a chef or a mechanic. As far as my parents' generation was concerned, Negroes were certainly coming up in the world and were in danger of forgetting their place. To the horror of my elders, and some of my contemporaries, they started to play baseball, go to college, become lawyers and doctors, and want to send their kids to our schools and live in our neighborhoods. Any day now I expect to hear someone say right out: "You know, it's getting so that it just doesn't mean anything to be white."

Which is just the point. It doesn't. And it never should have. And it is probably going to continue that way, not only with race, but with nationality and religion and a dozen other labels. We are all going to have to stop getting basic meaning and identity out of life from labels that are superficial and sometimes only "skin-deep." Now I want to be sure that I am not misunderstood. I am not saying that religion or country or race are going to lose all meaning whatsoever. They will always form a large part of our identities and be sources of personal inspiration and comfort to each of us.

What I am saying is this: the universal ingredient and force which permeates all life—namely, change—is changing for the faster, and this means that it will become more and more necessary for each of us to be more resilient and flexible, more spontaneous in dealing with the new and unforeseen, and it will become less and less easy to find security and stability by just adopting the traditional customs and ideas and attitudes of the past. As an example, watch this coming election year and pay attention to those who use race as a crowbar to pry open the white race's fear for its future. And watch those candidates who talk about America and Russia as if they were two static, antagonistic civilizations that never change or shouldn't change because one is always on the side of God and the other always buddy-buddy with the devil—and you will see what I mean. For you will see men and women who are trying to stem the tide of time by leaving time itself, by going outside of time. Only Dave Brubeck can do that. These are people who fear change and people who fear reality, which is really saying the same thing.

If one wants to avoid change, that is, escape from reality, one must avoid time. For there can be no change without time, or at least there can be no way of measuring it; best of all, if one is unconscious of time, one can be oblivious to change.

But if Einstein taught the world anything, it was that time is relevant to everything—and therefore so is change. To fail to see this is to deny the mechanics of life on this planet, indeed, in this cosmos. To see it and to deny it is to react to a tidal wave by turning our backs on it.

I wonder how many of you in the first graduating class of this school named in his honor know that we honor him not only because he was a mathematical genius but because he was also a truly profound humanitarian? He was truly brilliant as well in the field of human relationships, keenly aware of our limits and capabilities, insightful as to the nature of our dilemma, concerned that we progress personally as well as technologically.

Besides, I have thus far only offered you an unsolved equation or, better, I have only told you the factors that do not fit the equation of finding stability in our changing environment—or perhaps we should say finding permanence in our environment of change. I ought now at least try to tell you what factors I think do fit the equation. I would like to see if we cannot find in his life and thought these very factors. For I believe Albert Einstein was the kind of man who possessed just the qualities we all need if we are to face the rapidly changing world about us without overpowering fear, but rather with a sense of integrity and purpose.

If you were to read through any of the several volumes of Einstein's ideas and opinions, you would, I think, immediately see four personal qualities that stand out in bold relief: firstly, his refusal to live in an ivory tower; secondly, his appreciation of the mysterious; thirdly, his honesty and humility; fourthly, his refusal to rely on appearances alone. It would be interesting to speculate as to what extent these attributes enabled Einstein to gain that special insight into our physical world which he has bequeathed us through his mathematical formulas and scientific papers. For tonight, however, let us be content with seeing how such qualities might enable a human being to view the personal world—the world of people, oneself, and one's relationship to others.

One of the great stereotypes of our time is that of the professor or teacher or scientist who lives in an ivory tower, pursuing a field of study isolated by high walls of test tubes or books. Albert Einstein did not wall himself in. One can read volumes of his letters and articles written on the most important political and social issues of the day. As he became more renowned throughout the world he became in fact more involved throughout the world in the major causes of the world, especially disarmament and peace. Often he would write to high officials of different countries directly. Throughout his life he remained with the world, involved, concerned, speaking out.

As he said near the end of his life: "I have expressed an opinion on public issues whenever they appeared so bad to me, and so unfortunate, that silence would have made me feel guilty of complicity." This was an echo of what he had said previously, almost a decade before the Eichmann trial and Hochuth's play "The Deputy" made us all aware of guilt by silence. In 1950 Einstein asserted that "external compulsion can, to a certain extent, reduce but it can never cancel the responsibility of the individual." History records that Einstein was forced to leave Germany by Hitler because he was a Jew, but I wonder if he wasn't forced to leave also because he refused to make his digits and symbols into an ivory tower from which he would not notice the rise of Fascism in Germany.

As we all know now, many were those who did make their life's work, their business that is, their occupations, into their ivory towers. The construction of ivory towers is not found only among scholars. Anyone who uses what they are doing—job, bringing up children, going to school—as an excuse for not becoming involved in the crucial social issues of the day builds an ivory tower; in other words, ignores reality and turns their back on the tidal wave of change. But of course the wave of change hits anyway and engulfs them, tossing them about in such a way that their tower becomes their tomb.

Thus the first factor we see in Albert Einstein's life that satisfies the equation of unsure human beings facing constant change is that we must put ourselves in a position where we can face change. We must not wall ourselves in, or avoid being moved or touched, or be motivated to keep silent. Before any of us can face change with security, with integrity, with purpose, we must be willing to become involved, to become concerned, and, like Einstein, to speak out when moved.

Now we might ask, "But isn't it natural to be afraid out there, outside the tower?" The world is so big and so unexplored, so much is unknown, so much beyond our control. Did not Einstein feel that way too? I do not myself really know. I do know though, I think, why he was able, in fact delighted to face the unknown. And this is the second personal quality of Einstein's that will enable us to face change, namely, his view that the most beautiful feeling we can have is the mysterious. For him it was the fundamental emotion, which stood at the cradle of true art, true science, true religion. Encountering the unknown did not frighten Einstein; it thrilled him. It uplifted him; we might say, it "sent" him. In his own words,

> Whoever does not know mystery and can no longer wonder, no longer marvel, is as good as dead, and his eyes are dimmed. A knowledge of the existence of something we cannot penetrate, our perceptions of the profoundest reason and the most radiant beauty which only in their most primitive forms are accessible to our minds—it is this knowledge and this emotion that constitute true religiosity. In this sense, and in this alone, I am a deeply religious man.

Einstein was unafraid of change because he was willing to adventure, willing to discover, willing to find out, and willing to find that he could not find out. And this is the second factor which helps solve the equation of man and change. To be willing to face change you must be willing to accept—indeed find fascinating—the complexity of the universe, in the stars or in a snowflake, in your feelings or in your thoughts. If you want to remain inside of time you must be willing to be perplexed, confused, dumbfounded, thunderstruck, awed by the mysterious in life.

But now we come to a very crucial point. To admit confusion is to admit imperfection, and to admit the mysterious we must also admit human limitations on knowing, sensing, and reasoning. And this is the third factor in Einstein's personality which fits our equation. Einstein, this great genius of our times whose very last name has become synonymous with magical mental powers, was the first to admit his own human limitations. One might think that the person who is best able to face the unknown is the one who is most sure of himself. You might think that the person who is least afraid is the person with the fewest doubts.

But I wonder. I wonder if the absence of doubts or the presence of sureness is really indicative of a desire to encounter change. For how could such people admit the mysterious? Einstein was a very humble man—and by humility I don't mean self-abnegation. And he was a very, very honest man, and by honesty I don't mean merely not telling lies. His humility and his honesty were two sides of the same coin, the coin which constantly bought him passage into the world of the unknown. His writings are totally lacking in pomposity, his apologies for what he has failed to do always sincere.

His doubts were often public knowledge. When he felt he was on slippery ground, he said so. When Einstein was heaped upon with honors, he was still able to hold his head up to see the worth of others.

He once wrote, "Let every man be respected as an individual and let no man be idolized." He saw the divine aspect, the holy part, the untouchable portion of every human being, and yet he also knew that no human being was God. I believe that this so very brilliant man was able to make use of his brilliance exactly because he also knew he could never know everything. His knowledge of his own limitations as well as his own capabilities encouraged him to make use of those abilities, and in the long run they became the honest critic of his own accomplishments. After all, a god in the world of men is doomed to a life of boredom.

This then is the third factor to satisfy the equation of unsure human beings in a world of constant change. Not to face the world as a god but as mortal, neither all-knowing, nor all-powerful, nor free of death. On the other hand, when once willing to admit that we are mortal, willing to adventure and willing to be awed, then we are capable of having knowledge, power, and life.

As I am sure many of you know, before Einstein physics seemed almost always to square with common sense, with what anybody might have guessed had they really thought about it or had the proper tools. The twentieth-century revolution in physics of which Einstein's ideas were so much a part taught us that reality was not always as it seemed. A ruler might be shorter if you moved faster, time passed at different rates depending on where you were standing, light can be bent by gravity so the stars aren't really where you see them, and matter could be created and destroyed or at least transformed into energy and back because they are the same thing in different forms. The universe is expanding, without limits: there is no end to space, or at least it is receding faster than you can reach it and might as well be infinite.

Einstein's refusal to rely only on what appeared to be true, or common sense, or what society believes, or what the previous generation taught as if it were divine wisdom, correct for all time, carried over from his mathematical ponderings to his attitude toward life in general. In a letter he wrote to a schoolgirl, he freely admitted that many teachers did not take kindly to him. He himself had trouble in school! He was too independent. He was certainly no model student, he said, and they were always passing over him when they wanted assistants.

In later years, his social philosophy embodies this principle of independent search for truth beyond what society or its leaders say are right and wrong. As he once put it, only the individual can think, not society. Thus Einstein saw that, whereas in the world of physics, law was reality as well as a system of order, in the world of human beings, law was only a guide and of little value if the spirit of tolerance did not hold sway. Indeed, when that spirit of the mutual respect for the rights of others was not there, he supported those seeking their rights to go beyond the law: thus he did with conscientious objectors who refused to serve in the military, thus he did with Gandhi, who freed 400 million with his passive resistance, and there is no doubt that had he lived, he would have supported Gandhi's present disciples led by Martin Luther King.

And so, the fourth factor. If we are to keep up with change, we cannot rely solely on appearance—not in the world of physics, and not in the world of people. If we are to face change with honor and integrity and purpose, we must question appearances and look beyond them. We must ask ourselves whether they exist because God made them that way and thus they are part of reality, forever, or whether they are man-made and thus measurable by time, and susceptible to change.

Change is changing for the faster, and you boys and girls are going out into a world so dynamic that it will leave you breathless, as it already has your parents' generation. Who of us can control this whirlwind that swoops down and sweeps up, and places in new relationships to one another some of our most cherished ideas and fundamental beliefs about race and religion and nationality, and ultimately about ourselves? We must either stop the clock and live without reference to time, so that the nineteenth or the fifteenth century are not separated from the twentieth, or we can learn how to live with the ticking.

I suppose that among the high schools in town there are the usual rivalries and the usual claims about which school is better. I honestly do not know where Einstein High School ranks. But I do know this: throughout your lives, as you think back about your school, its name should be more beneficial to you than the memory of a place or a ranking or a team score. It should remind you of a human being who, among all the equations he solved, also solved the problem of human beings and change. He did not make his life into an ivory tower, but became involved and concerned with the world about him. He did not fear the unknown, but found the mysterious to be one of the most fundamentally beautiful experiences we can encounter. He did not lose confidence in his ability to meet the future when he admitted his limitations, but accepted them as part of the reality of being human. And he did not assume that any idea or attitude or law of physics or of society was right just because of its age or the number of people who subscribed to it.

May his memory be forever a blessing.

Stop and Go

An address to the young people of Bethesda Jewish Congregation

I know that none of you young people here tonight have ever driven an automobile, except perhaps in your daddy's lap, but I imagine that all of you have driven in automobiles enough to know some of the rules a driver must follow. For instance, you all know that a red light means danger—stop—and a yellow light means caution—slow down—and naturally a green light means go ahead, still, of course, with caution, since one should always, to use a well-known phrase, "be prepared."

You are all familiar with these rules because not only people who drive must follow them, but also those who walk; and while you are not yet drivers you are already walkers. Now, just as with the drivers, you walkers oftentimes come to a corner where there is no light. What do you do when there is no signal to tell you what to do or guide you? For, after all, the lights do not really make you stop or be careful or go; you must make yourself do these actions. The lights are there to guide you in making the right decision, but the real responsibility for your actions comes from inside you.

What do you do then, when you must take on this responsibility without the guidance of these lights? Well, I guess we can say, you use your judgment. You look carefully, and, on the basis of your past experience, your brain says to you: "I must wait," "I must be especially cautious," "I can proceed."

Now all of this is really pretty obvious; isn't it? Who doesn't know what red, yellow, and green lights mean? Who doesn't know that at corners where there are no lights we have to make our own judgment take the place of these lights? But how many of you have ever thought that all of growing up, and even after you are adults all of life, involves knowing what to do when there are no lights around to guide you? All through life, all of us are constantly coming to and turning corners with no mark, or signal of any kind to help us decide what to do next: to decide if that is a place to stop, to be especially cautious and slow down, or to speed up. All of growing up is concerned with learning to make those red, yellow, and green lights flash in our brains even when our eyes really do not see them.

I think you would be surprised to see how much you have learned already to see the red and yellow lights flashing in your mind. I do not include the green light because, surprisingly enough, it is the green light that is most difficult to do without, and not the red or yellow. But I will come back to that later.

About the red light: when you want to eat something new, you always look on the label of the container to see if it is good for you, or if it is old, or just plain poison. After a while you get to recognize certain wrappers; some that are particularly attractive remind you of a good taste, and some that have a skull and crossbones staring you in the face say to you stop and put it back. And so the wrappers act like traffic signals. But, really, if you came across a piece of candy in the street without a wrapper, you wouldn't need a signal to tell you not to put it in your mouth, would you?

Likewise, there are many other things which no one has to tell you not to do for you realize it is wrong—I'm not saying, now, that you will not go ahead and do it anyway. But suppose you were playing in the street, for example, and a stranger came up to you and asked you to take a ride with him, or offered you something to eat. He might seem very nice and you might really want to accept his offer, but I am sure a loud bell would not have to ring or a big light flash to warn you that a stop signal is needed here. Or in school, you do not really have to have a little signal on your desk to flash red every time you are impolite and annoy a neighbor or teacher. In all these cases you have already grown up to the point where something inside you tells you what is right and what is wrong, when to go ahead and when to stop—without needing some signal at each crossroad of decision.

Caution lights, like the stop lights, also flash within us. You hear people talking and you are bursting to say something. It is rude to interrupt, so you wait for the proper moment to begin talking. You are swimming and begin to feel tired; something tells you to slow down. You are playing with your friends, doing what they do, then they plan to do something you do not think is right: you should not need a yellow light to flash and say, "Caution, don't just go along for the sake of going along." You have some work to do, maybe you haven't practiced yet, maybe you have to meet someone—but you're having fun and time is running out; you should not need a flashing light to tell you: "I had better slow down, I had better not do anything more or new, I had better be cautious and watch the time."

At first, our parents and teachers act as our traffic lights. Gradually, we begin to have our traffic lights built in. That is called growing up. And when we show that our own light system is working well, our parents begin, more and more, to let us make our own decisions, and they begin, less and less, to worry about our ability to take care of ourselves.

But the green light, ah, this is a very special and difficult case. For some reason, it is easier to know when to stop than when to start. It is easier to know when one definitely should not cross the street than when one definitely should. If there are cars coming, there are cars coming, and that's all there is to it. But even if there are no cars in sight, one is always liable to come speeding along or rush out from a driveway. Our parents spend a lot of time teaching us when to stop and when to be cautious; that is, when our red lights and yellow lights should flash. But they do not teach us much about when to go ahead. No one can really signal you at just what moment to become interested in something, at just what moment to stand up and defend your rights, at just what moment to begin to help someone in trouble. All three of these situations are matters of individual, personal decision. They are more than just questions of right or wrong, or of what is harmful or not. In such cases, you must each develop your own green light to tell you when to speak out if some fellow student is being wronged by the others, or if some friend makes a nasty statement about Jews or Negroes or Catholics or any other group of people. You must develop your own green light system to tell you when to help in time of need, when to run for help, when to yell fire.

If you came to a busy corner and spied a silver dollar across the street, you might need a red traffic light to remind you not to rush carelessly to the other side. But you would never need a green light to tell you: "Go after the coin!"

As you grow older, you will find more and more things that you want to go after, more and more streets that you want to cross to reach one goal on the other side. Sometimes you will need your parents, and teachers, and elders to take the place of those red and yellow lights to guide you and protect you from rushing too quickly and harming yourselves. But you should never need anyone to act as a green light to tell you to go after what you want, to tell you what to do with your life. And what you want to do with your life, what you go after, is worth a lot more to you than a silver coin.

"A Reason for Living"

Diary from Hebrew Union College, 1954–1955

* In the fall of 1954, Edwin Friedman entered the doctor of divinity program at Hebrew Union College in Cincinnati, Ohio, after his graduation from Bucknell University. It was the oldest Jewish seminary in the United States and the main seminary for training rabbis, cantors, and educators in Reform Judaism. These entries chronicle Friedman's desire to pursue the rabbinate and describe the emotional fallout from his father's death from hypertension, which happened just months earlier, on the night before his twenty-second birthday. Written from the point of view of an intellectually empowered young man, the journal also gives the reader insight into the genesis for theories that later become the hallmark of Ed Friedman's thinking. We have only the diary covering his first year; he was ordained in 1959.

OCTOBER 19, 1954

Tomorrow is the beginning of the beginning—a new experience. It will be five long, long, not too easy years. So far it has been fun; so far there have been no classes. I went to my first Simchas Torah celebration at Ohav Shalom.[1] Danced, sung, and drank, left early, though, with my shirt wringing wet. Shouldn't have left because I got into an argument with several boys who have been here a year. And I started it—I don't really know why I said what I did, namely, "You know, I think some of the guys around here don't believe in God." I really was surprised to see how personally they took it. Think I did it because inwardly, after six days here of just seeing everyone have a gay old time, I wanted to get out of the intellectual desert. Anyway, there is no doubt that I meant it. Though I still understand why I only argued halfheartedly. Maybe it was because I realized that it wasn't worth arguing with them. One sees immediately that one must decide whom, during the next few years, it is worth arguing with. Moreover, I don't want to develop the ridiculous reputation of acting like I know it all. I really have to laugh when they tell me, "Don't think you know it all!" Would I be here if I did?

Have thought of another reason why I may have gone back to Judaism and decided to enter the rabbinate. It was a desire to identify myself. A realization that individuals do little for anything or anyone. It is only when they take a stand, when they identify themselves with some philosophy or institution. Sure, I had the ideas and the ideals, and I could have even woven them into a systematic philosophy, but it would have been an unmoored philosophy drifting in the passage of history.

I conducted services at the home for the chronically ill before ten very old and sick people. It was pathetic and yet inspiring. At first I felt odd about thanking God for his mercy and his care as I looked over "my congregation." But then I thought of how long they had lived. . . . Moreover I don't think I could ever stay in a blue mood for too long again if I can recall that scene. I have two hands, two legs, two eyes, two ears, a nose that smells and breathes, a mind that functions, a mouth that eats and talks, and I can control them. There is order within me; the same order with which I was created.

---

1. Literally "rejoicing with the Torah," Simchas Torah is a celebration marking the conclusion of the annual cycle of public Torah readings and the beginning of a new one. It is the only time that the scrolls are removed from the ark; worshipers leave their seats to sing and dance with them for several hours.

OCTOBER 20
Had my first day of classes today. It is going to be rough as hell.
Will have little time to waste. . . . Want to write Mom every day; it
would be such a lift for her, but keep telling myself that it really isn't
that necessary since I call on Sundays. I want to hit myself every
time I say that. . . . True, there is not that much to say. But when I
think of her coming home from work in the evening, what a home-
coming it would be for her if she knew there would be a letter waiting for her all the time. How quickly I have forgotten or, better,
neglected the vow I made at the bier of my blessed father. I am still
the romantic. I would not tell them, but I don't think anyone else
here cries as they translate the Bible. Especially the Isaac–Rebecca
romance, and of course also the Jacob–Rachel. Yet neither story can
surpass the pathos, the charm, the beauty, the complete submission
to the other, the blind obedient love that characterized the marriage
of my parents. May it only be so with me and whoever I shall marry.

OCTOBER 21
I make snap judgments about people, although I do not stay with
them for long. But how well I do judge at first sight! I noticed it especially at Bucknell and likewise here. It is very useful. But damn it,
I am nowhere when it comes to judging girls. This undoubtedly
stems from some bad experience I had in the past. I don't trust
them. I am eternally aware of the gold digger and me with no gold.

Oh God, how much I want to have an object for my passion,
how much I want to love. That is all I would ask you for myself. All
else which I ask, that is, what I want that might help me in my drive
for the rabbinate, is really for your glory. My love too will be for
your glory, but I have no power, or at least feel no power, over getting the object of my love. I do feel the power to be, with your continued inspiration, successful in the rabbinate.

NOVEMBER 1

Cried last night about Dad for the first time in a long time. God, how Mom must suffer. There was a family. Were ever two people more in love? His death was a tragedy in the fullest sense of the word. He had all the great qualities a man could possess which might make his death a tragedy. He was proud, for good reason, he had courage, and he could feel sorry. God, he could love. Then maybe it is our society which is the tragedy. For it taught him to express in such horribly material ways his so un-horribly non-material emotions. Am keeping better now the oath which I took at his bier. I think I broke it within two months after his death, and continued to do so, till I got away here. But seem to be more capable of at least fulfilling my mother's life when I am away from her.

. . . . How much more one gets from the Bible when reading it in the Hebrew. Funny, but since I have started reading Hebrew vocally, and using a few expressions, I have lost much of my miserable New York accent. The quality of my voice has really changed.

The two most powerful lines I have yet found in the Bible are as follows: When Rebekah is chosen as the wife for Isaac and is asked by her father and brother if she will accompany the servant to her new home, she answers their question of "Will you go?" with simply "I will." Here is the symbol of Jewish love, the symbol of love in the family out of which I sprouted. Love deep, obedient, unquestioning, committed.

And the other statement just as obviously appeals to me because of my past family experience. It is when Joseph places his two sons in front of Isaac for his blessing, and he, thinking of how he had long thought his favorite dead, and then finally finding his son alive, and actually seeing his children, says, "I had not thought to see your face again and lo, God has let me see your seed also." My father wished two things in life—to see my graduation and my seed. He missed both. But he enabled both.

NOVEMBER 7

The euphoria continues. I am elated by what seems to be a combination of enjoyment of the present and love of sad memories of the past. All of which helps one to live, wish, will, or whatever you want toward a very happy future. My sad past is, of course, my father's death and the destruction of a home of love, at least the destruction of it as it existed then. But perhaps it is nothing more than a reformation: I am at last giving forth that love out of which I was nurtured and matured. I have little to feel against anyone, and so much to feel toward so many.

. . . . What determines the successful rabbi? The size of his congregation, the size of his temple, the size of his paycheck? The amount of words he has after his name in *Who's Who?*. . . Judaism does not stand for bigness or, as Heschel[2] so greatly puts it, "thingness." It is, as he says, a religion of time, and thingness destroys or rather takes one's mind off time. Our whole society in its fear of time wants thingness, and the rabbi who agrees is not a leader. He must be teaching things that are different from what society believes in, or there is no need for him. He is just a back slapper, and a soul drowner.

. . . . Am more and more sure that a great deal of the disharmony here is due to sexual frustrations. So far I have been fortunate. But see, I am really worried that it will end, and so am plotting what to do about the infantile game of going steady. Funny thing is, I cannot make up my mind about my true feelings toward Stella.[3] Everyone tells me I have the belle of the town, and so I should not worry too much about grabbing too fast before I have a chance to meet others. Although I know I did grab out of the fear that there would be no others. . . .

---

2. Abraham Joshua Heschel, author of *The Prophets, Man Is Not Alone,* and other highly regarded books, taught at Jewish Theological Seminary until his death in 1972.

3. The young woman Friedman was dating at the time.

NOVEMBER 14

Isn't it unbelievable that a person should think so immaturely, know it, and yet be unable to stop it? I am in an interesting, if not terrifying, situation. But it can be so much superior to that of all my classmates. Within one year, as plans go, I will be the only unmarried student in my class. (There is one more, but at this rate it does not look as though he will stay long—I must talk to him.) So combine this with the fact that it is almost impossible to find a decent girl in Cincinnati, and I am going overboard to go "steady" (it's an awfully awful word) but I want the security, maybe, of just the sound. On the other hand I do not want to go overboard with anyone, because of past experience. I am very afraid of being hurt again. Not to mention all those I have hurt.

It is undoubtedly good that I shall not try to take Stella out next week. It is good for me to try to meet one or two others—this is the mature way of talking. After all, I do not want to get tied down. I have this singleness and should take advantage of it. I can go around the country this summer and around Israel next summer. That is the long-range view, the mature perspective. Only we live in the immediate experience. I guess that is maturity, to be able to live constantly aware of the relationship of your immediate experience to the eternal, and to be able to think and act in terms of how the immediate affects the eternal. That is not only emotional or social maturity. It is religious maturity. For is not the eternal, God?

I have become far too calculating. I plot and think out everything I do. This is fine in the intellectual realm, for ideas must be thought about. But not, at least to such an extent, when dealing with other people, or *myself.* It is leading me to a determinism that can only lead to pessimism. Reading and discussing Freud has affected me too much. For by my very nature, I am constantly trying to figure out reasons for everything I do—but worse, everything I have done.

DECEMBER 5

Well, it's been a hell of a long time. Too long. I have just kept putting it off and this is destroying the whole purpose of keeping the
diary.... So I might as well start with what happened today, and
keep going back, and in the future write more often, a little each
day. I bugged up as usual with my love life. It is amazing, but that
is the most immature phase of my existence. Or perhaps it is just
that in that phase of my existence, my immature qualities show up
best.

Namely, impatience. I have always wanted to go steady like
many of my friends, but I never have. Somehow things never
worked out right. Of course I did spend four years at Bucknell,
where there were few girls whom I would have even liked to ask out
more than once. This whole desire to go steady is really a drive for
security. It's funny that talking with Bob today, he said that I should
try to find this security in creation. For I do have a fantastic imagination; I only wish I could channel it. But that takes practice and
I am too impatient. I want to write and I have so many ideas; I want
to create. But I am lacking discipline, and I keep wanting to go out
on dates weekends when I should stay in and write and create and
imagine.

This episode with Stella has been very revealing, although it is
unlike anything that has happened to me before. The facts seem to
be that I met her, wanted to go steady with her immediately because I wanted to go steady, and she seemed to be right. Therefore
I rushed too fast, asked her out for whole weekends, but never said
anything definite to her that would make her feel I really loved her.
On the other hand, because I never came out and said anything definite, she undoubtedly became utterly confused. Now it is certainly
not for the girl to bring these things to a head, and I was of course
too weak, so today she asked me to come over and to reveal how I
felt. The poor girl was really suffering and it was completely my
fault.

Now why did I act this way? Undoubtedly my father's death and
living away from Mom for so long made me feel the desire for a

companion in whom I could confide and feel more than a friendly relation. Moreover, I frankly did not know how I felt toward her, thus I kept hoping that I loved her even when I thought that I didn't. This explains why I never told her that I plan to go to Israel after my second year. I was afraid that if I did, this would prevent her from ever falling in love with me. Anyway, today was a catharsis. I hadn't realized not only how much I was cluttering her mind, but also how I was confusing and adding unnecessary difficulties to mine.

Finally, she is a wonderful girl. She is still very young and emotionally immature, but every now and then she emerges from her cocoon of adolescence and speaks with the maturity that can only come from an eighteen-year-old girl who from the age of three to twelve was brought up in a Catholic convent with her sister, who did not see her parents (because they were separated and fleeing the gas chambers), and who was reclaimed after the war, not wanting to be Jewish, but becoming so after fleeing with her parents again from the Russians. . . .

In closing, I am still as optimistic as I was when I came. I still feel in the same state of euphoria. And I have less doubt than ever that I have chosen *the* (I cannot bring myself to say *path*—right path, that is)—strike *the*—I have chosen something for which I nor any other Jew will be sorry for. Least sorrowful of all may be God.

DECEMBER 9

Is impatience the root of immaturity, or is it the root of something else? And what is immaturity the root of? Better, what causes immaturity? What causes impatience? Finally, what is immaturity?

These traits come out most obviously in my affairs with women and in my study habits—or better, only in the latter when the former affects them. For instance, let us take the mood I am in now. I have a test tomorrow, but really do not need to study much, one or two hours would take care of it. Thus I could have much free time tonight and this, added to the weekend coming up tomorrow, gives me the potential of much time to do the many things I want to complete, nay, start. Yet as I walked up the stairs from the dining room and happened to glance at the snow blotting out the few black patches of road left, and as it drifted slowly, lazily past the light on the outside wall below the window, I received a tug in my heart. I wished to have a girl to love at that moment. I think perhaps I am jealous of the rest of the boys in my class. I want so to have someone to love. Yet is it not possible that when my love comes, although it will be the last, it might well be the strongest, the most reciprocally faithful? Staying in such a mood of dreamful romance, of course, hinders my ability to create, to study, and yet it is only through study that I may be able to stay out of these moods. What the hell is my hurry? Mom used to say to me, and still does, that I want to learn by injection—not so much that I want to sit there and have it shoved into me without my doing any work, but that I am in such a hurry to get it all. . . .

At this time (that is, while I am typing these thoughts) I think I have gotten past the immediate, the impatient, the immature. I have taken cognizance again of the goal I want most out of all that I wish to do. And then, too, I am listening to music, the Beethoven violin concerto, to be specific. What would I have done all these years without music? How it has dragged me from morbid depths. Of course, I no longer go into these periods of depression, but how it takes me out of the immediate. I do not mean that it provides a means of escape, but rather that it prevents me from escaping.

Let us try to be very specific. I am currently sorry that I do not have one particular girl whom I like very much and who returns such favors. I have no one to share such joys as I might accrue from funny or interesting experiences, from creative experiences. Moreover, with wanting to do so much (I am such an extreme extrovert) I need more of a discipline, at least in time. That is, I need a schedule, but a schedule based around periods of release. Periods of release that I do not have to look for, but that I know are there for the asking. I want, in a sense, security, and this despite the fact that I am completely sure that the rabbinate is what I want to enter, that I want to serve Judaism, the Jewish people, God.

Now, is it not possible that I might meet such a girl tomorrow? I could go to Hillel. But that is impatience. For I would like to read and write tomorrow. Besides, for now, for the next two years, I must plan on everything as it falls into the perspective of my spending a year in Israel after the completion of my second year here. It is only after that time that I will really want to get married.

I guess I want to have my cake and eat it, too. I want to have a life filled with both learning and love. But I want it now. And how few people get it at twenty-two; indeed how few people get it at all. I am sure that I eventually will. I have made a covenant with God. But just by procrastinating and wanting to have such a girl now, I am almost breaking the covenant. For sure, I am not showing faith in it.

NEW YEAR'S EVE, 1954
Well, I shall spend the last thirty-six or so minutes of the most eventful year of my life (so far) in retrospect. But I shall, of course, make no resolutions since I am sincere in what I am about to write. Within the space of one year I pulled out of the hat of experiences the trick that will awe me for the rest of my life. Out of all the interests that plague any extrovert, I did not choose one on which to guide the rest of my life. Oh no, that would be too conventional; I chose them all. That is really the choice of the extrovert: he must pick one out of the many or find an integrating factor for them all. Of course, there are so few integrating possibilities. I remember last New Year's Eve so well. My father was dying in his room (unknown to me, of course, at least as to the nature of his condition) and I sat here in my room writing a chapter for my research paper for the State Department. Some time during that evening I mentioned to my mother the thought of becoming a rabbi. I am sure she took it not too seriously. I wonder how seriously I took it. When I look back now, realizing how much I want to be a rabbi, how much I realize that the rabbinate means for me the association of my drive, my thoughts, my feelings with a force that gives them meaning outside of myself, I keep saying to myself, how lucky I am that I came upon it, that I went through with the applications and the interviews. I say all this as if I felt that I really was not too enthusiastic

or sure about the idea this time last year. And yet at the same time I sometimes say to myself, how could it have been anything else?

. . . . Last April, during the first rehearsal for *Othello,* I did not get the lead but had one and maybe two other good parts. I was just beginning to feel aesthetic elation in being in a Shakespearean drama. I was just beginning to feel the beauty of the language and to feel part of the tradition of English literature (of course I was working backward, since I started with Sir Peter in *School for Scandal*) and I was called home for the first of two times to my father's bedside. The rest of the semester was a nightmare. But I didn't crack, damn it. And when I returned to Bucknell with three weeks to graduation and fifty thousand words' worth of papers to do, I had some pretty tough weeks in there, torn between my father's certain and yet uncertain death and waiting to hear if (really, *when*) I would be accepted for the rabbinate. And slowly I lost a father and gained a reason for living.

. . . . It could well be that this next year will be more important. It does not seem possible that it should be more fundamental. The groundwork has been laid. . . . I have so many ideas for writing, and I have so many things that I want to read. If only I could prevent myself from goofing off. It is again the question of maturity, particularly of discipline. I must use my individualism to remain aloof from those things that I know will keep me from doing what I want, which will consume time. I must make little projects out of what I wish to learn. Set up little goals, such as writing one particular story next, or reading one particular book next, or learning one particular ritual next, and I must stick to each until it is finished before I go on to the next.

. . . . Why is this night different from all other nights? Because the law allows liquor to be sold all night in New York. Because one can get shickered as hell and be publicly condoned, because one can blow his fool head into a fool horn, and most of all because unlike all other nights in the year—it falls between the day of December 31 and the day of January 1. So you other nights shouldn't be jealous at all. You too have your uniqueness.

Psychologically, I guess, New Year's is to the year as the sabbath or the weekend is to the week. One has made a big deal of it so that one can have something to look forward to besides death. Man just cannot go on doing his regular routine without having some marker in time to give him the illusion that when he reaches it, he can "start over." Thus he gets over his rough spots.

JANUARY 3, 1955
(Continued from New Year's Eve—a little more introspection)
Last week I did something which, as a child, I imagined would be the most dread-filled experience one could encounter. I went into a cemetery alone on a dark, gloomy day. I drove around looking for my grandparents' graves, feeling sure all the time that I had very little gas left. (As it turned out I had plenty, but nobody could have guessed it from the gauge.) I have decided that is the only time to go to a cemetery—alone, and on a day when the atmosphere can squeeze from you the emotions proper to the occasion. The week before when we went to visit Dad's grave, of course I did not resent going with my mother, and not just because I knew I was a comfort to her. But I did resent the presence of my kindly aunt and uncle. There are times when one just does not want company, no matter whom.

It was the same feeling that drove me back to the funeral parlor to bawl at my father's bier after we had all left it for the evening. Of course, maybe it is just that I feel I am too big to cry in public and it is just social pressure that holds me back. I am sure this is a factor at such times. But I am also sure that one is better able to feel as he wants when alone. Let's face it, man, I am pretty close to a mystic. My imagination enables me to conjure up all sorts of closeness to the dead who are my beloved. It was five years since I last visited my grandmother's grave and many times during the interim I thought of how I would enjoy going back alone. And I did—I enjoyed it. Not just the peace and serenity one can gain from being engulfed in rolling hills of slender, quiet, rain-dripping moments, but almost a division of my soul and body in which my thoughts and feelings go forth to encounter the memories of bygone memories and come back refreshed, pleased, and then quieted.

I did not make a vow, but I shall do all in my power to remember to bring back at least a handful of dirt from Israel to place on the grave of my grandmother. She wanted so to go there (maybe in order to be buried there). I will never be able to ascertain how much the little stories she used to tell me about Poland, her childhood, and the sincere warmth that characterized her desire to visit the Holy Land all gathered within the folds of my brain to emerge at just the right time later on, and to lead me to the choice I have made.

FEBRUARY 10

I really did not study for that final. Oh please, God, let me pass and go on to other courses! I promise to work hard just to get ordained. I have made a distinction: I want to be a rabbi and to that end I must be ordained, pass courses, etc. But I also want to be learned. And I must never confuse ordination from Hebrew Union College with being a learned rabbi. If only I did not have to spend all this time looking up words.

I want so to go to Israel, to get out of the complacency and the "positive thinking" of this immature, emotionless materialism. At least as an ideal, that will be my home. On the more practical side I will learn enough of the language to make the course easier and give me more time to study. I sit here listening to Hillel and Abiva and I just want to go. Not in my most ecstatic moods over Beethoven's *Ninth*—moods which kept me going all through Bucknell—have I ever felt the emotional attachment to the music itself as I do when hearing Israeli music. I feel myself carried out of myself and into my people. I have such a longing to go there. Oh God, I must not wait too much longer.

And I must decide if I shall live in my native land. Indeed, I must decide what shall *be* my native land. I had thought that if they wanted me to take Hebrew over again, I should try to make them see that I really do know enough stuff to go on. And if they would not listen, I have contemplated both Jewish Theological Seminary and just going to Israel and getting out of this whole mess, but I feel I am just running away.

. . . . My love life is still as piss-poor as ever. Why can't I find a girl to go steady with? It is that simple and just as childish as I have expressed it. I keep saying that I do not want to get married until after I go to Israel, but I need so badly to have someone to love, that I can feel, and that I can feel loves me.

FEBRUARY 27

Somewhere, I imagine, when I was much younger, or perhaps all throughout my life, I have gotten some pretty stiff blows to my pride. I can remember many of them. That I have always tried to be different is probably something I seized upon to make myself feel I was recognized. I can remember always rooting for the visiting team when I went to ballgames with my father, and he called me contrary Ike. . . . Never have parents been so good and tried so hard to bring up a well-balanced, normal child.

. . . . Now the fact that I have always been very tall has set me apart from any group I have ever been initiated into. There were other incidents, such as wearing glasses that made me see worse. Or being made nauseous easily in day camp. All through my life I have been different—but the significance is that I have reveled in it. Of course, I revel in it out of necessity, the fact that I have no choice. And since I am different, I might as well enjoy it.

My relationship with girls has always been strange. I have in most instances found it difficult to make advances. Why, I don't know. I remember my mother always giving me lectures on premarital sexual relationships, but this I don't think was the deciding factor. Sam may have hit it square when he said I was afraid of being repulsed. In fact, I know I have said that to myself before. But of course this is a flight from reality, and to keep up a real relationship with a girl on such pretense really makes a neurotic out of one.

On the other hand, it is not my general nature to be afraid to do something at which I am afraid I might fail. And I never cease to use myself as the butt of a joke, so maybe this is not the deciding factor in my attitude toward sex.

Sam's suggestion as to the way out is religious. To say that it is faith in God would convey no meaning at all, although this is what it essentially is. But for six months now I have been writing a paper on my God concept, and I have unfortunately so intellectualized him that I have almost forgotten how to feel him.

Yet I remember the night we stopped in West Virginia, the night before I came here. I went for a walk and had a religious experience. I made a covenant with God, as had my fathers. I said I would be the most sincere rabbi imaginable, that I would study very hard. That I would devote my life to Him and to Judaism. I wanted only one thing in return—I wanted a wife. I wanted someone devoted to me, someone who would share with me my experiences.

. . . . So now I think I love Hatsie, and I say it with the greatest care. [4] I don't want to go overboard. I have been hurt too much in the past. Why do I think I love her? She is a real person and there are no airs about her whatsoever. She is interested in the beautiful things in life. She is truly spiritual, truly humble. She is, of course, sweet. She is not beautiful, but I am sexually attracted to her. She is an individual. She is a human being: she is compassionate.

So what do I do? Do I tell her how I feel about her? Have I given her enough time to think about me? Am I too impatient again? Am I perhaps taking a risk on losing her with my bad timing? Is there such a thing as bad timing?

I have to make a decision here. I am afraid of bringing it to a head for two reasons. First of all because if I do, and she does not love me, or we have to stop seeing each other, I am afraid that there is no one else. That there could never be anyone else like her. This is of course the madness of the moment.

But more important (is it really?) is the fact that I am afraid that after only dating her five or six times, it is not fair to make her start thinking so now. And indeed the same questions asked a month later might provoke a completely different response. The only way out is faith in God. If I have made this covenant, and have tried to live up to my part of it, then I should have no fear. But do I have faith in the covenant? Do I have faith in God? Do I believe in God?

---

4. Hatsie Brav was the daughter of a Cincinnati rabbi who served as a mentor to him during this period.

Well, I do. But I am not sure that this ineffability I call God is to be prayed to in such a situation. Whether prayer in such a situation does any good. For if prayer must be accompanied by action, what shall be my action?

APRIL 29 *(although it really doesn't matter)*
My God! I always thought they joked about people in love wanting to write poetry. I feel as though I wish I could pour my whole soul, my very essence, into a cup and give it to Hatsie. Never have I been so completely overwhelmed by anything or anyone outside my own existence. I have sat here and worried for weeks whether this "infatuation" was just another infatuation, to which type of feeling I have always been so prone. And yet now, now it seems that there can be no doubt. Yet there is. Will there always be?

Or is there a doubt? If I do love her so, if I am not deluding myself, then what the hell are we waiting for? As I lay here just now, I thought to myself of telling Hatsie there can be no doubt. As for me, this is it. But to what end? Suppose she agreed!

For years I have always thought that the time might come when I would be going with a girl and it would come into my head to ask her to marry me, or we would just get to the point where we would agree it was a strong possibility. But all that time in my thoughts it was always some romantic dream in the future. And so no matter how deeply I became woven into the pattern of my dream, no matter how completely detached from the real world I became, and how completely immersed in the projections of my mind, I never in all the world thought that when the moment came, that all those dreams would not be an escape but the very core of reality itself, that when such a transformation came—I would be scared stiff.

It was so easy in the dream world to feel nothing but the romance idealized. For in my dream world there was no doubt that this was the girl I would marry. For had I not created the dream world, and no less the girl? I had created the girl I was going to marry and so I had certainly not created one about whom I could have any reservations, nor one who would have reservations about me. But it is not that I have so many reservations about Hatsie—indeed, any—it is myself that I have reservations about. For in my dream world I too was perfect. For had I not created myself in my dream world?

And so here I am back to the beginning, or maybe the end. My metaphor holds. I am living at a time in my life where every trite cliché that I have ever heard come dripping out of jukeboxes and Broadway shows and movies has suddenly lost its triteness. And maybe this is the test. For the newness of the situation is what has made the staleness of the platitudes evaporate. And it is only a new situation because I have never truly loved like this before. Indeed, not just these gushing words about idealized romantic love in America have become refreshed, revived, but life itself has taken on a completely new meaning.

.... It is interesting that I have not made an entry here in so long. Many times I thought of it, and it is true that never have I had so little time in which to do it. But if I really had wanted to, I would have. And this brings up the question of why the diary itself. Was it really because I just wanted to keep a record of the many ideas that came into my head all day, and which I thought would someday be worth remembering or elaborating upon? Or was it just the need to write?

Or are all such ideas merely rationalizations for the true subconscious purpose for which I was driven to keeping this record—for the sake of unraveling myself, of seeing myself, or getting to know myself? Or instead, was it just loneliness caused by my father's death and being away from Mom at the same time? Far away with no particular friend?

I am not lonely now.

MAY 8

At this point I feel so confident in my ability to be a good rabbi, to teach, to get people to enjoy listening to me. Frankly I had no idea that I would be able to teach kids so well, to get them to like me so well.

I must go to the high school next week regardless of whether or not Hatsie can go. I owe it to the kids, to Judaism, to God. They want me, and since they feel the way they do toward me, I can do some good. In a larger sense it means that I shall have confidence for the great job I have this summer teaching at the camp in California.

Certainly was an interesting talk I had with Hatsie last night. It has revealed to me how young she really is, how long it will take before she will be steady enough, emotionally mature enough to want to get married. She is still too extroverted. I think I gave her a really good metaphor for how she will have to look at this. She thinks she loves me, but she can't imagine settling down with anyone or imagine anyone putting up with her for a lifetime. Also she has never met anyone with whom she thought she could keep her interest for a lifetime. She is afraid of losing her individuality, of giving up some things through marriage.

It was the same thing with me when deciding on a vocation. I could not decide what I wanted to do, and if I did finally come down to teaching, what to teach. There were always so many things that would be excluded by my choice. But then when I finally made the choice, I was surprised at how many things were not excluded and even more that the things I had to exclude did not mean so much to me after all—in the light of what I would be doing, with whom I would be, with what meant most to me in life.

She will have to decide that too, or there will be no marriage for her. She will have to begin to feel toward someone in a way that those things which she feels marriage will prevent will seem very unimportant in light of the one she wants to marry. And, oh God, may I be that man.

It takes time to make good wine. Our relationship, as close as it is, must mature much more. We are both very complicated people and for that will both have to spend much time with one another.

It is really interesting to compare our relationship to other couples who are getting married. Some of them have only known each other as long as I have known Hatsie, but since they have already decided to get married they can't understand when I tell them it is no use for them to keep asking me if I am getting engaged. That it will take a long time for it to happen, if it is going to happen at all.

~

MAY 26

Oh, dear God, tradition has it that on this day thou gavest the Torah—indeed, life—to your people. I am a member of that people, oh Lord. I will be a leader of that people, oh Lord. Oh Lord, give me the courage to be a leader, to lead and not to follow. Give me the insight to know how to live and not become involved in its petty quarrels, to rise above it. To teach, live, and love Judaism. This first year has proved to me that I do love Judaism, that I want to live Judaism, and that I can teach Judaism. It is so interesting, dear Lord, that instead of being so broken up over this blow that I do not want to lead services at the Old Folks' Home tonight. But I do want to— in fact I look forward to it with the utmost enthusiasm, as a moment of praying and of thanks. And, dear Lord, I do not mean to bother you so much for this one point. But I want so badly to love someone, to have someone love me, to share my experience with someone. To be married. Oh dear Lord, please forgive me for this conceit, but as I look around this college, I realize I could be wrong on every point of my intellectual analysis. But I am not wrong on my attachment to Judaism, on my love for all that it means to me. I therefore offer to you in return for your Torah one thing: sincerity and a complete submission to your will. But if you want me to attain my creative fulfillment through that sincerity and complete, obedient love, then you must give to me what will help me to achieve the goal of being a teacher in Israel. I want your love, oh Lord, as manifested in a wife, and at this blind moment, as manifested in Hatsie Brav.

Three Marriage Sermons

Given at Bethesda Jewish Congregation

Sometimes when a couple seems to match well, we say they make beautiful music together. Actually music and marriage are very similar. For to create beautiful music is not an easy task. Melody requires inventiveness, spontaneity, sensitivity. Harmony requires depth of understanding, adaptability, constancy. Yet even the most beautiful melody in the world, if left alone, loses its beauty to the boredom born of repetition. Having lost its freshness because it has become too self-reliant, it is unable to evoke new imagery—one soon tires of it and is no longer moved by its tones.

Likewise the most versatile bass, the one richest in warmth, capable of the enhancing support which pretty melodies crave, often appears, when unaccompanied, to be but a series of disconnected, uninteresting, purposeless sounds.

And yet—if the melody and the bass are skillfully blended together—they make music wondrous to hear. The melody, though played repeatedly, is then fresh forever, and the bass—even the same bass is forever new.

Yes, music and marriage are very similar. They are both the blending of the light and the heavy, the sharp and the flat, the harmonious and the inventive, dissonance and chords, with the final result depending always on sensitivity and depth of understanding.

The harmony of marriage is also a blending of beauty and of strength. Though the harmony of marriage is a harmony of counterpoint, each part, the treble and the bass, must be self-sufficient and have a right to exist all by itself. And yet despite this individuality each part must feel free to draw upon or give to the other. And sometimes it is permitted for the treble to be strong, and for the bass to be carefree—indeed, sometimes the rhythm of life demands it.

May the composition of your marriage be sweet and stirring, may its rhythm be harmony, and may its music enrich your lives.

There are many human happenings which seem to be the result of chance, and marriages seem so more than any other. It is a watch running slow, a knock on the wrong door, one's old friends, one's job, a last-minute decision to go somewhere else that allows two people to meet, to talk, to love, and to marry.

This chance meeting that is so often the beginning of a planned eternity has always been pondered by Jewish people. One sees it in the literature of long ago, in the story of a Roman woman who comes to two rabbis and asks, "So what does your God do now that he has created the world and set it in order among the planets?" And the rabbis answer: "He matches up couples." "Is that all?" she said. "Why, I could do that myself." "Maybe so," the rabbis retort, "but for him it is as difficult as splitting the Red Sea."

Thus has our heritage tried to say to us: do not make light of this "chance," nor take for granted this opportunity—as one might when given a surprise business offer, or upon accidentally overhearing about a good restaurant, or when one comes suddenly upon an old friend. This is the opportunity, this is the chance—if it is accidental as all that.

And so I would ask you to ponder a moment as you look forward hopefully to the morrow and the establishment of a home in Israel. That you ponder a moment whom you might thank for this gift of love and this joyous covenant. You are about to share fully one another's lives, the sorrows as well as the joys. Remember that the home you build, unless it is established according to the plans of him who laid the foundation, is labor in vain. Hallow your future lives together with faith in one another and approach the marriage altar with understanding hearts.

   May peace ever dwell within your home, contentment, love, and joy within your hearts. May you grow old together in health and never neglect this opportunity, nor him who arranged it.

Since I have known you both barely one year in this past twenty-five which we are celebrating tonight, I shall confine my remarks largely to the next quarter century. And since I am closer in age to your children than to you it would be chutzpah for me to speak either as one who welcomes you into a select club or as one who hopes to enter it soon himself.

   As I propose this toast to the next twenty-five years, I hesitate to mention your names individually and thus separate you into two distinct persons. For surely all that each of you has done for others and all the happiness you have shared together is because there is in each of you a part of the other, and each of you is all the more for that. Besides this reciprocity, however, there is another reciprocal relationship regarding marriage and it is to the fruits of the second that I shall address the toast.

   For if the first reciprocal relationship is that between husband and wife, the second is that which exists between the couple and those about them. What they have given to others and what others have given to them. But at this point the two reciprocal relationships interconnect. For even as each has given more because of union with the other, so will each rejoice more in the return of what they have given because of that same union.

   Speaking then more as a son than as a friend, and more as a new friend than as an old acquaintance, I think of the return that awaits you because of your past investments—and here of course I mean your investments of time and energy and emotion.

   As you watch your children marry and raise their children, and as you see our congregation develop into the center of Judaism you wish it to become, may you reap the well-deserved harvest of the love and care you have planted, and may these next twenty-five years be filled with the joy and comfort of personal achievement and the gratitude of others for the joy and comfort you have given them.

Part Two

THE CHALLENGES OF MATURITY

The Joy of Discovery

A sermon preached at Temple Shalom, Chevy Chase, Maryland, on October 13, 1963

Columbus Day honors a great discoverer and, in honoring him, honors discovery itself. It honors a great explorer and in doing so honors exploration. For they cannot be separated, discovery and exploration. One does not "come upon" if one does not "venture forth." What is revealed to us in life is rarely found just because it is there. Were it otherwise, mankind would have perished long ago for want of being moved. The exultation that we feel, the joy that we experience when something is revealed comes only because we would explore.

How fitting then that Simchat Torah, a festival when we honor the Torah, should fall on Columbus Day, too. For is not this festival, called the Joy of the Torah, also an occasion which honors discovery, which honors revelation? And it also is a day which honors exploration. For we do not honor the Torah merely by dancing or parading with it up and down about the altar. We also read among its words, from the last and from the first, as we begin again to explore and uncover anew. One might say that the Torah gives to us what the sea gave to Columbus—the opportunity to explore its depths and breadths, its beauty and its mystery. We cannot "happen upon" what is in the Torah any more than Columbus could have "happened upon" America. As he did, we have to venture forth if we wish the *simcha* of revelation, the joy of discovery. After all, it is only because we have throughout each year made such explorations that we experience such joy in its discovery. Were we to leave the Torah as an idol in the ark, there would be no such *simcha,* no joy. Indeed there would be no revelation, no discovery.

Let us realize, then, that the joy of discovery is not only for those who climb the highest mountains and search the farthest horizons. If Columbus and Moses seem to have been the great explorers of their day, we mustn't think today only of the John Glenns and Matthew Shepherds who navigate the macrocosms of the sky or of those who search the smaller worlds of positrons and cells.

The joy of discovery is not limited to them any more than exploration is! Have you ever wakened earlier than you usually do and gone out to walk earlier than usual about the neighborhood in which you live? And have you ever noticed how all the colors and the shadows and the shapes of all the things you know so well are as if newly discovered? How everything that you have seen before—a house, a street, a lamp, a tree—is as if revealed for the first time? How wondrous becomes the unseen when seen, the unexplored when explored, the undiscovered when discovered?

The joy of discovery is part and parcel of experience itself. Each life has its own horizons, its own beauty, its own depths, its own frontiers. One need not be the pursuer of grandiloquent tasks to taste the joy of revelation. That joy can always be found, but it will not come to us unless we are willing to explore. What better lesson is to be learned from our Torah than that it opens itself up to everyone who would explore it. And so it is with all of life, at work, at home, and in solitude.

At work the joy of discovery comes to those who explore new and unforeseen ways and methods to do their jobs, although what they do may seem routine and not susceptible to change. At work it comes to those who seek in everyone they meet the uniqueness that belongs to each, the way they think, perhaps, or how they laugh or blush or even how they respond to you. At work it comes from exploring our own reactions to another—a fellow worker, perhaps, or employer—to discover on what new planes we both can meet.

At home this joy of revelation is for everyone who sees a child grow up and learn to walk and talk, then to take his lead in investigating what is so obvious to us we never even noticed it. It comes to those who are willing to explore the world we have lived in so fast we never understood it. At home the joy of revelation is for those of us who would take notice of the bonds connecting us to those we love—and having noticed, seek to discover new ways and words for sharing who we are with whom we love.

And in our solitude the joy of discovery comes from what we've learned to do but never thought we would. It comes from trying—and from training. It comes from looking into who we are and growing into what we want to be. It comes from becoming. It comes from participating with the stars, the sunset, or with the autumn leaves and knowing the kind of sensations not even poets feel for somebody else. In our solitude, the joy of discovery lies in the exploration and the revelation of ourselves.

It would be misleading, however, to say that all such joy is unaccompanied by pain. Columbus did not glide across the great blue sea, feasting on delicacies with no fear that his boat would be becalmed. The astronauts are not chosen by chance but because they can withstand great suffering, and are willing to do so. Those who make discoveries that lead to better understanding of microbes and molecules are not rewarded on the first experiment. Nor do those who venture to understand the meaning of the Torah learn to read and write and think without privation and frustration.

In our own personal lives also, therefore, we must not expect the joy of discovery to come without the pain of exploration, the tedium of experiment, the frustration of human limitations, the conditioning of experience.

But the choice is not pain or joy; it is both, or else it is impassivity. As with Columbus, it is a choice of living forever in a world that is old or trying to discover one that is new. And as with the Torah, it is a choice of being satisfied with interpretations of an age gone by, or exploring the old for revelations that are new.

Systems and Ceremonies: A
Family View of Rites of Passage

Written for publication in Family Life Cycle *by Elizabeth Carter and Monica McGoldrich (New York: Gardner Press, 1981)*

Rites of passage are usually associated with emotionally critical moments of life. Yet most studies of these ceremonies have tended to ignore the crucial role of the family at such events. The convention in the social sciences has been to place primary focus on the culture which provides the rites, or on the individuals who are being passed through to a new stage in their life cycle. The role of the family at such occasions has tended to be seen as secondary, as occupying more of an intermediary position between the individual members to be passed and society. From this perspective the family participates in the customs provided by a culture as a way of helping its members take their new position in that culture.

Twenty years' experience as a clergyman and family therapist has given me an almost totally different perception of the role of families in rites of passage. I have found that the family, far from being an intermediary, is the primary force operating at such moments; primary not only in that it, and not the culture, determines the emotional quality of such occasions (and therefore the success of the passage), but also in that it is the family and not the culture that ultimately determines which rites are to be used. For families are far less determined by their culture's customs and ways of doing things than they are selective of, according to their own characteristics and pathology, their culture's ceremonial repertoire.

Of course, the family will always say, "That's just the way we (Jews, Catholics, Fijis, Aborigines) have always done things (at our weddings, funerals, baptisms, bar mitzvahs)." Indeed, so central is the role of family process in rites of passage, it is probably correct to say that it is really the family that is making the transition to a new stage of life at such a time rather than any one individual.

What may be most significant, however, in switching one's primary focus to the family is that it enables one to see the enormous therapeutic potential inherent in natural family crisis. For the one phenomenon which has stood out in my experience with families of all cultures is that the periods surrounding rites of passage function as "hinges of time." All family relationship systems seem to unlock during the months before and after such events, and it is often possible to open doors (or close them) between various family members with less effort during these intensive periods than could ordinarily have been achieved with years of agonizing efforts.

I believe this is true because with respect to timing, life-cycle events are not as random as they appear. Rather, they are usually the coming to fruition or fulmination of family processes that have been moving toward those ends for some time. Life-cycle events are always part and parcel of other things going on. They always indicate movement, and it is simply easier to steer a ship when it is afloat, even if it is drifting in the wrong direction, than when it is still aground.

The purpose of this chapter will be to explore three natural life-cycle events (death, marriage, pubescence) and then to comment on three nodal events which are less a natural part of the life cycle and more a creation of the times in which we live (divorce, retirement, geographical uprooting). I would like to begin by briefly mentioning three generally accepted notions about family life which I believe are myths and which inhibit forming a family process view of rites of passage, and enumerate four principles about the relationship of family process to rites of passage which are basic to understanding the conceptualization of my theme.

Three myths about family life inhibit the development of a family process view of rites of passage. They are:

(1) that the family is breaking down;

(2) that culture influences family process in fundamental ways; and

(3) that the rite of passage is the same as the ceremony which celebrates it.

(1) The notion that the family is "breaking" down is supported by the higher divorce rates and by the greater physical distance between relatives which is produced by our highly mobile society. That notion, however, is not supported by who comes to funerals, weddings, and bar mitzvahs. Nodal events in family life have an absolutely transporting quality, able to transcend great distances or gulfs. Sometimes it is only one or two individuals from another part of the country, but they are there to represent that part of the clan. Sometimes it works the other way, of course, and individuals whom everybody expected would come, don't, allowing the physical distance or the climate to be their defense. One member will have trouble getting a car out of the garage to drive twenty miles, and another will, on finding the local airport snowed in, drive 150 miles through a blizzard to another town, from whence he can take off. Nor can one always predict, based on previous relationships, who will do what. There is also no correlation between the distance family members have to travel and their punctuality at the ceremony. If anything, there is sometimes an inverse ratio.

It is possible, of course, to say that all this is proof of the breakdown of the family and the underlying need for family relationships. It may not be all that accidental, however, who appears at which event, and the therapeutic potential inherent in bringing family members together at life-cycle events should not be discounted because of distance. A better metaphor for the present state of family life than a "breakdown" might be to say that the family has gone "underground," and nothing will coax various parts of it to surface like a rite of passage. The umbilical cord is infinitely elastic.

One cannot assume that the members of a family who are most distant from home base are those who are most necessarily independent, or least reactive emotionally. Instead, they are often those members of the family who most need physical distance in order to relate with any independence at all to the family members back home.

For example, a woman has been maintaining an adaptive mode of relating to her critical husband in order to keep peace. She is visited by a sister whose presence makes her feel less alone, or the opposite, a mother whose dependency requires a lot of thought and emotional energy. In either case the homeostasis of her marriage will be upset and the husband, feeling the withdrawal of emotional energy, now perceiving his wife to be less cooperative or less attentive, becomes more critical than ever. Actually, I have found it a general rule of thumb that when one marriage partner is visited by relatives, the other often becomes more reactive during the stay.

Such phenomena can occur at any family get-together, and probably helps explain much of the increased anxiety around Christmas. (See below the comparison in family process terms between Christmas and bar mitzvah around the issues of drinking, gift giving, and suicide rates.) But at family rituals which are associated with nodal events in the life cycle, the whole emotional energy system is higher to begin with, thus they are prime time for the confluence and the redirection of intensity. It may be more correct to say, therefore, that the major breakdown which occurs during rites of passage is not the family itself but the family's defense of physical distance.

(2) The second myth has to do with the relationship between families and culture. Rather than determining family life in any significant way, culture is the projection of family process on a societal level. To understand family life in general, through its customs and ceremonies, no less the emotional life of a particular family, is to engage in circular reasoning. Rather, culture is the medium through which family process works its art.

Thus while a strict Catholic family, a rigid Methodist family, or an orthodox Jewish family might claim they are only following their religion when they operate in a given way, the fact of the matter is there are very few families that observe all the customs of their religious tradition in the proper way. In fact, what culture has general agreement among its leaders as to what is right? Obviously one can often find other families from the same culture, if not members of the same family, who do it differently.

What seems to happen in family life is that individuals and families respond most strongly to those values which coincide with their own lifestyle. Every religious tradition and cultural background has its own neurotic usefulness.

There are some crucially important ramifications for the rites of passage of this reversal in conceptualizing how family and culture influence one another. The first is that it gets the therapist out of the middle between his client and his client's background when issues come up about rituals or ceremonies, and the client says, "I can't do that because it's against my tradition." Questions like, "Do all the members of your faith do it that way?" or, "Do all the ministers of your religion agree with yours on that issue?" can open the door. Sometimes one can go the other way and ask, "How does it happen that you are so strict (orthodox or observant) about this particular religious or cultural matter when you do not follow so many other basic tenets of your faith?" For example, to a woman contemplating divorce: "Well, I can understand your decision never to marry again, as a good Catholic, but how did you decide to go against the church on birth control?" It is not important whether or not they can make fine theological distinctions, but that they realize they are taking responsibility and thus in either case made themselves the final judge of who was to be judge.

It might be objected, "That isn't true on all issues—no orthodox Jew would ever sanction a mixed marriage, nor a strict Catholic, marriage to a divorced woman." First of all, that is not my experience. Loyalty to tradition does not seem to hold true when dealing with the complexities of family emotional systems at life-cycle events. Beyond that, however, what is important is not the position individuals take at such times, but how they function with that position. Even if it were true that an orthodox Jew is more likely to object to a mixed marriage, or an observant Catholic to marriage to a divorced person, the intensity with which they react is another matter and one that tells much about the family or their position in it.

For example, an objection simply stated as such, or even a refusal to go to an event because it is against one's principles, can be understood as a definition of position. On the other hand, cutting off, disinheriting, constant harassment, or heavy interference has nothing to do with cultural values and traditions, even though the family members acting that way may claim they are defending the faith. The roots of that kind of fanaticism will always be found in that family member's unworked-out relationships with their own family of origin.

It is just not possible to keep this kind of focus on family process clear as long as one assumes that family members' behavior is determined by, rather than selective of, cultural background. Actually, to the extent one can keep this focus clear, two other benefits accrue. First, it probably means that every time a member of a family gives a cultural explanation for why they do or can't do something, far from being the enlightening comment it appears, it is probably a denial of family process. From the therapist's point of view, therefore, rather than dutifully writing it down as one more significant datum, it should be recognized for the warning light it is about where that person is stuck in his or her own family.

The second benefit that comes with keeping one's focus on family process is that culture and custom can then be used as a tracer element for getting a better reading on family members' relationships with one another. Take, for example, five grown siblings in their fifties or later, only one of whom keeps kosher, or only one of whom is still a pillar of the local parish. You may safely hypothesize that this is the child stuck with the responsibility for Momma's memory. Noting such clues can often be helpful in understanding why certain family members are functioning the way they are during any rite of passage.

(3) The third myth inhibiting a family view of rites of passage is the assumption that the ceremony *is* the rite of passage. After all, some individuals are married long before the ceremony, and some never do leave home. Some family members are buried long before they expire and some remain around to haunt for years, if not generations. This myth has a corollary—that the members of the family who are the focus of the ceremony are the only ones who are going

through the passage. The whole family goes through the passage at nodal events in the life cycle, and the passage often begins months before and ends months after the ceremony.

Ceremonies celebrate. From an emotional systems point of view, they are not in themselves efficacious. Rather, their effect is already determined by what has been developing within the emotional system of the family. Ceremonies do focus the events, however, in that they bring family members into conscious contact with one another and bring processes to a head.

On the one hand, therefore, the celebration event itself can be a very useful occasion for meeting people, for putting people together, for reestablishing relationships, for learning about the family (both by observation and the hearing of tales), for creating transitions (for example, in leadership), or for the opportunity to function outside or against one's normal role, e.g., getting "looped" when one has always been expected to be the sober one. On the other hand, my experience with rites of passage suggests that the more important time for becoming involved with one's family is in the months before and after the celebration, using the event more as an excuse for reentry—though, naturally, the more one prepares the soil before the celebration, the richer the harvest will be at the event itself.

For example, it would be nice to use the state of flux in a family system usually present at a funeral to bring a brother and sister into verbal communication again. But this is more likely to happen at the funeral if one initiates communication with each of them while the family member to be buried is dying.

Perhaps the most important point to be made about distinguishing the ceremony from the passage is that the potential for change which I have found near nodal family events could not be that great if the event were merely the event itself. For if one can get things going right before any given ceremony, then all the natural healing processes which age-old traditions have captured in their rites of passage will take over, and, at the celebration, do much of your work for you.

Elsewhere I have been developing this theme for clergy of all faiths, suggesting that an awareness of family process can enable a minister to draw on the natural strengths in families to enrich religious experience. The idea is not to "psychologize" religion. Rather, when the clergy use their traditional role (not any modern pastoral counseling role) to facilitate the meaningful involvement of family members at life-cycle ceremonies, they are in fact allowing natural healing processes to flow and doing what religion had always intuited, but what in modern times has come to be called therapy.

As I often put it to couples worried about their relatives' opinions: if the family relationship system is not operating pathologically, and this marriage is only routinely upsetting to the balance of your family system, then you could even include a ritual murder and everyone will still probably walk out commenting, "Wasn't that a lovely wedding?" If, on the other hand, there are severe rifts in the family (e.g., mother and her mother or sisters, or in-laws), or if the marriage is particularly disturbing to the balance of the parents' marriage, then it is a different matter. For then no amount of precaution about doing the customs and ceremonies properly will shield one from the infinite capacity which intensity harbors for the manufacture of criticism.

The logical conclusion to be drawn from this is, if you're worried about the length of your gown or the shape of the baptismal font, go work on the "triangles" with your parents. In fact, you may never have a better opportunity.

The explosion of these myths leads to some very useful principles, which in turn lead to the observation of confirming patterns. For the other side of the notion that the rite of passage is more than the ceremony, and the individuals going through the passage are more than those identified with the ceremony, is the idea that rites of passage always indicate significant movement in a family system. Not only, therefore, can a family approach to rites of passage make them smoother journeys, the crises these events precipitate become golden opportunities for inducing change in otherwise stable pathological relationship patterns.

As mentioned earlier, family systems seem to unlock during these periods. On the basis of my widespread experience with families of many cultures, I would venture that the following principles are valid at all rites of passage for all families regardless of cultural background:

(1) Rites of passage are family events coming at the time they
do because of emotional processes that have been at work
in the nuclear and extended family.

(2) The ceremony or the event itself reflects the fact that
processes in the family have been undergoing change and
are in a state of flux.

(3) The ceremony and the time before and after it are therefore
opportune periods for inducing change in the family
system.

(4) There seem to be certain "normal" time periods for the
change and working through of emotional processes at
times of life-cycle transition, and attempts to hasten or
shorten those periods unduly are always indications that
there are important unresolved issues in the family
relationship system.

I will now discuss three natural rites of passage—funerals, weddings, and puberty rites—and give some examples of how a family
approach can make the passage less fraught with anxiety and even
turn it into an opportunity for helping the family in broader terms.
Then I will comment briefly on three nodal points in the modern
life cycle that are not as natural, but which are becoming so widespread as to approach traditional rites of passage in emotional significance: divorce, retirement, and geographical uprooting.

FUNERALS

I begin with an event which is usually considered to mark the end
of the life cycle because I believe that death may be the single most
important event in family life. Over the years I have seen more
change in families—marriage, divorce, pregnancy, geographical
moves, other deaths—occur within a year after the death of a family member than after any other nodal point in the life cycle. Another reason for beginning with the "end" is that this event,

especially if it is associated with a particularly important member of the family, can influence the celebration of other nodal events which follow. For example, at the first wedding, baptism, bar mitzvah, etc., following the death of a person important to the system there is likely to be a larger turnout than one might have been otherwise led to expect. And when that occurs, that phenomenon itself may give an indication of who is going to replace the deceased member of the family. On the other hand, it cannot be said that the turnout for a funeral is as likely to be influenced by the nodal events which preceded it.

Death creates a vacuum, and emotional systems, as physical systems, will rush to fill it. In the process, cutoffs between family members will begin and end, freedom and getting stuck will be the fate of others, shifts in responsibility are normal, and replacement becomes a goal for many. The fluidity of a system around the time of death is thus also greater, though not necessarily for an indefinite period. In other words, if one is going to take advantage of that period, the funeral, its preparations, and its "celebration" can be a crystallizing event. From the other side, where death is expected, while that may create more anxiety and pain for the family, it also offers more opportunity for change.

Six major kinds of opportunity become available during this rite of passage:

(1) the chance to take or shift responsibility;

(2) the opportunity to reestablish contact with distant relatives (or close relatives that are distant);

(3) the opportunity to learn family history;

(4) the chance to learn how to deal with the most anxious forces that formed one's emotional being;

(5) the opportunity to shift the energy flow among the family triangles that seem to resurrect themselves at such moments; and

(6) the opportunity to reduce the debilitating effects of grief.

This last has the character of a time warp, since it involves affecting what usually comes after death by how one works in the family before death. But it may be the most crucial one of all, and better than any other notion encapsulates the idea that a rite of passage is more than a ceremony. The basic notion is: grief is the residue of the unworked-out part of the relationship.

Several of these are exemplified by the following story in which I was contacted in my role as clergyman, but where I was able to use my knowledge of family process to try to let the natural healing forces released by rites of passage flow. A woman who was herself very involved in community mental health called and asked if I would be willing to do a "non-religious" funeral for her husband who was terminal and might die any day. The rub was, she didn't want him to know about it. He was a scientist and very a-religious, but she wanted to do this for her sons, nineteen and twelve. I replied that I couldn't agree to do a funeral for a man while he was still alive unless I could meet him. (Another reason is that secrecy almost always stabilizes pathology, and increases anxiety in a system. I had observed numerous times when the impending death of a loved one was handled in a hush-hush way and began to wonder whether such secrecy around death is in itself pathogenic or is simply symptomatic of the systems that produce candidates for therapy.)

The woman said that meeting her husband was out of the question, and I responded, "Think it over." She called back later that day and said she had indeed spoken to her husband, and he had agreed to meet with me. I told her that I did not want to meet with him alone, but together with her and her two sons. She agreed, but warned me that she did not want any therapy. I agreed, and said I would only ask questions.

The husband had just come back from the hospital to die at home. When I arrived, he was lying in bed, and while physically weak, was perfectly lucid. He had been a renowned scientist, an only child, about forty-six, and he kept a phone next to his bed so that when his aged parents called from the Midwest they would not realize how bad things really were.

The older son was there, but I was informed that the younger son, who had asthma, had been sent to his mother's mother. I began by telling the dying man (in front of his wife and son) that I had never met anyone who knew he was going to die, and wondered what he thought about. He responded in a self-denying way, seemingly trying to convey that he was approaching his end with perfect equanimity. I upped the ante, telling him that his wife had said he was a very non-religious man, and I wondered if he was now hedging his bet before he met his maker. He again responded lucidly and with a great sense of character, "No," he knew this was really going to be final. I then asked him what he wanted said at his funeral. He again replied with amazing humility that there was nothing particular about himself that he wanted emphasized.

As far as I was concerned, to this point all the questions were just "probing the line." I now turned to the son, and asked him in front of his father what he wanted said at his father's funeral. At this point, by the way, a fortuitous ring of the phone took mother out of the room; she never came back in. I proceeded to initiate a conversation of the most personal kind between father and son over the issue of what was to be said at the father's funeral. The man died the next day. The son, at my urging, wrote and delivered the eulogy, and the mother, several days later, sent me a long thank-you note and a copy of Kübler-Ross's *On Death and Dying*.

As a clergyman I had an unusual opportunity in this situation, but I think that what happened there, and had never happened before, could only have happened in that family during such a rite of passage. Such experiences clarified to me that many are the ways of encouraging such a process if you are "lucky" enough to be seeing a client when terminality hits the family. My own experience with the dying, the dead, and their survivors is that an individual is not dying as much as a member of the family, that is, part of an organism is dying. When this focus is maintained, as impersonal and cold as it may sound at first, many new ways of seeing things unfold. For example, I believe that where extraordinary efforts are made either to end the person's life to "reduce suffering" or prolong a person's life when they are biologically alive but existentially dead, the family is either desirous of rushing through the passage or fearful of entering it. In either case it will say something about that dying person's family and the importance of the person to it at that moment.

Such an approach also refocuses the so-called "ethical" issues around "the right to die."

There is another important way in which the focus on the dying person rather than the family misguides on this rite of passage; it requires that the dying person be *compis mentis*. In many cases, they are psychotically senile, unconscious, in a coma, in denial, or just plain hopelessly confused. In those situations, from the point of view of that individual person's existence, they might as well be dead. But that is in no way true from the point of view of the family. As long as a dying person is above ground, he or she is a live part of the organism. (Compare the extraordinary efforts to keep political leaders alive even though they are no longer capable of ruling.) Systems know the extraordinary significance of burial.

Recently I had the opportunity to put into practice much of what I have been preaching, when my own mother, who had been deteriorating for several years with advanced arteriosclerosis, went into her final decline. In August of 1977, my mother, aged seventy-nine, whose mental and physical condition had been deteriorating for several years and who had, throughout this period, had to live with a home attendant, fell and broke a small bone in her leg. Since she had almost no pulse below her waist, the cast almost immediately created a pressure sore which would have become gangrenous without constant attention. She was put in the hospital in an attempt to debride the wound and save her leg.

Since my mother had all but stopped walking anyway, the surgeon wanted to amputate. The decision would have to be mine since I was her only child and my father had died twenty-five years previously. She seemed no longer capable of really understanding what was happening. Remembering my mother as a person who did not give up easily, I stayed on the side of trying to save the leg, but I was already thinking of her funeral. What complicated my own ability to think clearly during this period was the incredible anxiety of her sister, who lived next door to my mother. My aunt was a severe over-functioner who had made it to her eighties by using her anxiety to get others to take responsibility. Throughout those last four months, she would constantly criticize the home attendant to me, and me to everyone else.

In an effort to defuse the intensity in the triangle between my mother, my aunt, and myself, I began to contact other members of the extended family whom I perceived to be in interlocking triangles with me and my mother or me and my aunt. I started a process in which I tried to establish or reestablish as many relationships as possible with other members of the family and close friends of my mother's all over the United States. I kept informing them of what I was doing and what was happening. I found great support in doing this; the process of involving family members at a distance also seemed to redistribute the guilt and the responsibility, spread the risk, and make me more objective about what was happening nearby.

For six weeks the situation stayed the same, and then, just as the doctors were about to give up and I also, I made one last attempt to break through to my mother, directly telling her I was giving up. To our surprise the leg began to heal and my mother was able to return home. However, shortly afterward, the visiting nurse tied the bandage too tight, despite doctors' warnings, and my mother developed gangrene. At this point positions switched, the surgeon now saying that my mother was so close to death that amputation would be an "heroic" act. Since I had done a lot of thinking about how unresolved attachment makes it difficult to let someone die, I had difficulty with this one. My aunt, who had from the beginning been against amputation, was still against it. I, however, made the decision for amputation on the ground that I could not let my mother's body poison itself when that was preventable; she would have to die "naturally."

After the amputation, she actually seemed to perk up for a while. Again, throughout this period, I stayed in constant touch with the family and friends, informing them of what was happening, but in each case, only after I made the decision. Throughout this period my aunt and those closest to her kept attacking me for my failure to put her in a nursing home much earlier where she would have been more comfortable (meaning *they* would have been more comfortable).

Shortly after my mother came home from the hospital, it became clear to me that her body had gone beyond all thresholds and

that the tidal wave of pressure sores erupting out of a severely
blocked arterial system was truly irreversible. I began to prepare for
her death and funeral. Then the same visiting nurses, severely chas-
tened by the doctors for their previous mistake and feeling anxious
about her condition, wanted to put her back in the hospital. Luckily, I was called first. For three years I had fought against much family pressure to keep her out of institutions. It was now clear that she
had less time left than it would take to reverse the process of her illness. With great difficulty I made the decision not to have her go
back in the hospital and die in the institution, but to let ill-nature
take its course. I stopped interfering. Within five days, she was dead.

I had prepared a list of family telephone numbers, and when I
received word of her death, I began to follow out a plan I had
thought out while my mother was dying. I called each relative to tell
them my mother had died, and took advantage of the natural rem-
iniscing we went through to make notes of what each person said
about my mother. At the funeral, I read a "family eulogy" which included my own remarks and those of the other family members.
Then I asked those present to add anything they wished. As for me,
after the funeral I felt so much confidence in my ability to deal with
acutely anxious crises, you could have come to me saying, "We have
to find someone who will chair a committee to make a decision
which, if wrong, will send the earth out of orbit," and I would have
replied, "I'll take the job."

Here are some things which happened during this rite of passage in my personal life and client families:

(1) Three years previously, I was cut off for one reason or
another with everyone who eventually came to the funeral;
now things had swung so far the other way that one cousin
even invited my whole family to stay for a visit.

(2) Another cousin, who had recently gotten married
unbeknownst to the family to a women he had been living
with for years, came and introduced his wife to the family
for the first time.

(3) Knowing how money channels are emotional channels,
and having seen so many families split up over inheritance,

I tried to use that phenomenon in reverse by giving the newlyweds my mother's furniture, which they appreciated greatly.

(4) I found myself able to go back to work immediately and with enthusiasm and no depression. I found, if anything, an increased sense of creativity and competence in my work.

(5) Among my family therapy clients, several families went into crisis around this time. As I saw it, when I learned to deal with the forces of anxiety that had made me "me" I inadvertently pulled out some of the supports with which I had been previously buttressing these clients in my anxiety over their anxiety. They almost all made leaps of growth as I responded without anxiety to their crises.

(6) There was also an interesting reaction within the small congregation I served and which I had helped to establish fourteen years previously. Annually, whenever contract time came around, I had come to expect some attack from the "loyal opposition." In the past, I often went to great lengths to refute their charges, motivated by anxiety over my own security. This time, however, their complaints, though not different in nature, seemed almost silly if not boring, and I did not take them very seriously. Within several months the few members who comprised the opposition for that year launched an attack on my functioning with more vigilance than I had ever encountered in twenty years of congregational life.

One last point. Twenty-five years previously, I had for several months helplessly watched my father slowly die in a hospital. I had not dared to take the opportunity to tell him what he meant to me, to discuss with him his impending death, or to function in any way that might have proved helpful to me or my mother after his death. The atmosphere had been overcast with anxiety and denial. His wake left a sense of relief that it was all over, but it was relief wrapped in confusion, guilt, and a pervasive feeling of something left incomplete. He had made one statement to me when it seemed he knew he was going to die, something enigmatic like, "Eddie, do what you want to do." That remark became over the years like some mysterious pearl of advice one carries away from an oracle, which one is bound to plumb and ponder for a lifetime.

On the other hand, after my mother's death, it was an entirely different story. Though she had been anything but concerned about my future—in fact she had been often bitter, complaining, contrary, and sometimes in the confusion of her senile psychosis a name-calling witch—I had a sense of completeness, fulfillment, and peace. Treating a funeral as a family rite of passage and making the most out of that opportunity for one's own differentiation is the only way I know to get completely out of that horrible, forever-after haunting dilemma of wishing it would all be over soon.

WEDDINGS

If death is the most portentous event in family life, marriage may be the most symptomatic, in two senses. First, my experience with many couples before marriage has led me to the conclusion that the timing of weddings is far from random. I have found, for example, that many couples either meet their spouses or decide to marry within six months of a major change in one of their families of origin. It is not that romance doesn't count, but simply that it isn't enough to move a relationship to marriage. Weddings can also be symptomatic of family process in that stresses surrounding the engagement and wedding preparation period seem to really make the seams show. This can be true with funerals also, but there are some major differences. More likely than not, death will have an implosive effect on a family, in which all the members pull together, even if after the funeral they fight forever over the inheritance. With weddings, one must decide whether to invite those one doesn't want to be with, and the burden of choice can become almost overbearing, depending on how many sides one is trying to please. Whereas with a funeral the need for comfort makes the closest relatives willing to be with one another, with a wedding the desire to be joyous makes some of those same relatives anathema. Another major difference between weddings and funerals is that in death one is dealing with the loss of an insider; with marriage, the problem is the inclusion of an outsider, despite the old saw "I am not losing a daughter but gaining a son."

There can be, of course, a light side to weddings—the obsessive concern with etiquette, the stupidity of some of the gifts, even the jealousy of who gets seated with whom, though, once again, when viewed in family process terms sometimes these little things carry more significance than we might think. Sometimes it is blatant, like the mother who, during the wedding, whispers to the bride as she partakes of the ceremonial wine, "Not too much now, dear." Similarly, a humorous but often significant warning signal is when the mother or father is the one to make first contact with the clergy—either because their son "works" or because their daughter lives in Alaska and "it would be a long distance call."

One of the aspects of family ceremonies which has always appalled me, yet also proved to me that the unseen family process has more power than the ceremony, is the loss of critical taste at family events. I have performed very sloppy weddings in the most uncomfortable settings (bees literally in my bonnet), and had everyone come up afterward congratulating me on the warmest wedding they have ever seen. But I have also been part of such anxious systems that even in the most elaborately arranged settings, the most eloquent homilies were ignored and I had all I could do to keep from inadvertently stepping on the bridal gown and tripping the bride.

As an opportunity for inducing change, I have found that the rite of passage surrounding a wedding is most propitious for redirecting focus. The opportunities for learning about the family and reworking triangles described with regard to funerals are there also, but primarily the time around weddings stands out as the time to redirect a parent's focus, and once again crisis is opportunity.

Though this is clearly the case, most couples experiencing difficulties with their parents over a wedding see this period as just something to be gotten through until they can get married and get away. This avoidance of the experience might be similar to cremation after a death. Of course, the real getting away only occurs if they use that period to develop more differentiation of self in the relationships with their parents. And again, couples who are experiencing pain at such moments (as with terminal deaths) may be more fortunate. Where problems arise in the family of origin during wedding preparations, the opportunities for redirection of focus are plentiful.

I have never seen a religious, social, or other issue worked out regarding marital choice where the efforts have been made directly on the content of the issue. For example, if mother or father are critical of the marital choice on the ground of different religion or social background, efforts to change the parent's mind by saying things like, "But Mom, you were always so liberal yourself" or, "Dad you always taught me to treat everyone equally" are doomed to failure. Over and over I have seen a bride or groom spend an entire weekend with critical parents showing them the illogic of their ways, return thinking they have changed their minds, and then receive a letter later in the week showing that they are back at ground zero. These efforts to deal with the content of the parents' complaint are ineffective because one is dealing with symptoms, not cause. The cause of almost all severe parental reactions to marital choice is the failure of the reacting parents to have worked out something important in other relationships. The focus has been misplaced. On the other hand, I have found almost 100 percent success in reducing the significance of such issues, if not eliminating them altogether, when the bride or groom is able to refocus the reacting parent on other relationships: their own marriage, but particularly their own parents.

There are three major factors always present in the reacting relative's position in the family. One, he or she is having great difficulty differentiating him or herself from the child getting married. Two, and not necessarily distinct from one, the child getting married is very important to the balance of the parents' own marriage. Three, that parent or relative is always caught in some emotionally responsible position in his or her own family of origin.

There is little question that the third is most important, but it is also often the most difficult to get to. Some moves I have found helpful in numbers one and two are: "Well, Dad, it's all your fault, you should have sent me to Hebrew school (church on Sundays) more often." If the response is, "We tried, but you wouldn't go," the point is carried further. "Well, you were the parent, why didn't you try harder? It's a good thing your mother isn't here to see this." Or, for interfering mother telling daughter what to do at the wedding: "Mom, here is a list of one hundred aspects of the wedding; I know how important it is to you to please your sister (mother, mother-in-law, friends); would you look it over at your leisure and give me as full answers as possible? I am particularly interested in knowing whether you want the traditional approach to putting the knives next to the spoons, or the newer idea that the knife should be in front of the plate." These won't bring complete change, but they sure bring breathing room.

One, however, has worked without fail. It goes something like this: "Mother, I know you are opposed to John, and you have a right to your position, but you are still my mother and I believe you owe me one more thing before John and I marry. We have never had a frank talk about sex. What has been the secret to your marital success? How many times a week would you say a man likes it? And when you don't want it, how do you keep a man away?" I have yet to find a better way to refocus a parent on her own marriage, because parents satisfied with their own marriage just do not put that much energy into their children.

Sometimes a wedding gives one the opportunity to go to work in the primary triangle with mother and father. The key to any triangle is not to get caught in the middle as the focus of an unresolved issue between the other two. If one is caught, not only does one have less maneuverability oneself, but the other two wind up with a pseudo-stabilization of their relationship. One of the best ways to get "de-triangled" is to put the other two members of the triangle together. This is true whether the triangle is classic, as with an extramarital affair, or whether the third member is a symptom (physical or emotional) or one's partner, parent, or child. By seeming to encourage a togetherness which really has more appearance than substance, it is often possible to make the hidden issue surface where it belongs. (Anyone who doubts this should try the opposite, namely, separating the other two persons, or the other person and his symptom, and watch them respond by absolutely falling in love with one another.) When a person getting married can avoid the content of the objecting parent's remark and concentrate instead on the emotional processes of the triangle, that bride or groom will become de-focused as a natural part of any new process which now focuses the parents on one another.

For example, usually it is Mother who tends to be more reactive about a marital choice or over wedding preparations. If this turns out to be the case, and Dad starts reacting also, then one has a wonderful opportunity to tell Dad how terrific it is to see the way he stands up for her even when it goes against his principles. If it is Dad who is the primary reactor, and Mother won't stand up to him, similar statements can be made about how true she is to the old-world standards of the adaptive wife. The key is to keep pushing them together and praising their togetherness as one goes along.

There is also an obverse side to this triangle. This occurs when the parents agree to come to the wedding but very reluctantly, conveying that they are only coming out of a sense of duty. This is a trap. Here they have again put the bride or groom in the middle by making their child responsible for their behavior. Under such circumstances they will come with a vow not to enjoy themselves (which can be infectious). They will stay to themselves in a corner, perhaps with a sibling, standing like gaunt, Midwestern farmers from a Grant Wood painting, adamant against a smile. The de-triangling here involves making them come for themselves by giving them permission not to come: "Dear Folks, I know you are only coming to please me, and I don't want to see you give up your principles just because I am your favorite. I would like you to be there, but I'll understand if you can't make it."

A typical pattern that often needs addressing is the parents' reference to their own extended family. In my experience, when the parent says, "My parents are upset," that has always been a projection; likewise, when they say, "This will kill them," I have never seen the grandparent react more than the parent, even when their old-worldliness would lead one to expect more reaction. This is just more evidence that the issues have to do with the closeness of the

relationship, not the subject of the issue. In all events, the following letter has excellent success in my experience:

> Dear Grand... or Aunt or Uncle:
>   As you may have heard [they probably haven't] I am
> going to marry a Jew [a Catholic, a Black, a Martian]. I
> would like to invite you to the wedding even though I
> know this probably goes so much against your principles
> that you may feel you cannot attend. I did want you to
> know, however. Also, I wondered if you could give me
> some advice. Your daughter [or kid sister, not: "my
> mother"] is absolutely off the wall about this. She keeps
> telling me this will be the end of our relationship, calls me
> every night, says if you found out you would drop dead,
> etc. I wondered if you could give me any information that
> would explain why she is behaving this way, or any advice
> on how to deal with her....

My own experience has been that whenever that type of letter has
been sent, no reply is received, but within weeks the issue has
calmed down. Sometimes the unresolved issue behind a parent's reactivity near the rite of passage of a wedding has to do with a relationship between a parent and a relative who is dead, e.g., their own
parent, a spouse, or another child. When this is true a visit to the
graveside with that parent can offer an opportunity for unlocking
fixed attitudes and enabling refocus. The key, however, no matter
which way of refocusing one chooses, is that an impending wedding is already a sign of a relationship system in flux. Some members are going to feel the pull of the forces of change more than
others. Who is going to react most? It depends on who stabilized his
or her own life through some kind of extraordinary emotional de-
pendence on the person getting married. For example, some parents use a child as an anchor to keep from getting drawn back into
the vortex of the parents, or they invest in a child to compensate for
the absence of affection in a marriage. The road to no-change at such
moments is to elope, cut off, or try to placate the parents as much as
possible until one gets married and can start one's own family. Those
latter approaches guarantee a transference of emotional intensity into

the new family being formed. But where individuals can be taught to seize the opportunity at the rite of passage of a wedding, they leave a lot of unnecessary baggage at home.

Here is a clinical experience and a short case history which illustrates to how deep an extent the wedding as a rite of passage is a family event. A divorced man came in to get married who mentioned in the premarital interview that he was not going to keep up with his young child from the previous marriage since it would "complicate things for the child." I gingerly mentioned that by doing this he might create ghosts. But he didn't buy it, and I didn't pursue it. I did have, by the way, the impression that it all somehow had to do with his mother, who was not coming to the wedding. In all events, after the wedding he refused to give me my fee, saying that he had only come in to get married, not for counseling. It was the only time that had ever occurred, and I made a mental note that I had touched something deep.

Several years later a groom came in with the identical situation. Remembering the first experience and being a fool rather than an angel, I told this man what had happened the previous time I raised such an issue and added, "I know this must be a touchy subject, but have you thought about the possibility that for all your good will, your child might grow up wondering why her natural father rejected her by cutting off in such an absolute manner?" And I mentioned how often I had done family histories with adults who reported similar situations about their fathers or grandfathers who became ghosts in the system, and the residue of guilt those cutoffs had left behind to haunt the family. He laughed about the first groom, but said he simply didn't see it my way. Two days later, he called to say they had decided to get married by someone else.

Several years after that a man came in to get married who happened to mention that after several years of cutoff he had just reestablished relationships with his children. I said, "Oh, then you must have made some major changes with your mother." This time the groom looked at me as if he had seen a ghost, and responded, "How the hell did you know that?" I am still not sure how I knew other than to say that whenever a relationship changes suddenly near the rite of passage of a wedding, whether it is a cutoff or the reestablishing of a dormant relationship, my experience has taught me there is usually a third member of the family who is part of the triangle. The wedding as a rite of passage is like the movement of an iceberg, with most of what is in motion unseen by the human eye.

The second story is about a family of four children in which the eldest came in at age thirty-nine for counseling for her second marriage. While very well-educated, she was the black sheep of the family. Her father, a very successful tyrant, had died several years previously. The family, that is, mother (and one unmarried brother in particular), were in a fury about her marital choice, threatening to disinherit her. In a session with mother and daughter, the father's constant beatings of this daughter came out. Though she had had a lot of therapy all through her childhood, she found the subject very painful. I asked her at this point if she had ever seen her father's beatings as symptomatic of her mother's closeness with her. Her chains disintegrated before my eyes. She became motivated to lead the family instead of fighting it. For two months before and six months after the wedding, she went to work on every triangle with every sibling and her mother and relative she could find.

Mother, who around then had been shown great attention by a man for the first time since her husband's death, was told not to marry this man, that he was not good enough, etc., and what would her mother (now in her nineties) say? The brother who had inherited the father's super-responsible position (and who had not come to the wedding) was repeatedly complimented for being willing to give up his own personal happiness in order to keep the family together. Both relationships almost immediately began to shift. It was almost as though they were now seeing this woman for the first time. It turned out that the other brother, a flaky Ph.D. in his late twenties, was between jobs or hobbies, and youngest sister was an absolute slave to her rigid husband, with physical symptoms beginning to show up in one of her children. Every one of these dysfunctional symptoms which had been helped to operate covertly through the perpetual focus of the family on "poor sister" became approachable again, as if for the first time, around her wedding.

Putting to work all the energy and intelligence characteristic of the family, which had been allowed previously to intensify pathology or to become sopped up by rebellion, the black sheep used the opportunity made possible by the fact that the family was in the midst of a rite of passage to de-focus her scapegoat position, and everywhere, the family began to change.

PUBERTY RITES

The third universal rite of passage is that of puberty, the onset of adulthood. Of the three, this one has lost much of its family significance in modern culture, becoming associated often with cultural phenomena, graduations, dating, etc. My own religious tradition, of course, has maintained it with the celebration of the bar (boy) or bat (girl) mitzvah. I would like to shift gears in this section and talk within my own tradition's metaphor about this rite of passage.

The major reason I wish to stay within my own tradition on this one is that I have experimented with changes in the tradition based on what I have learned about family process, and the results so far have been both astounding and enlightening. What I wish to show is first, how something as obviously individual, no less child-focused, is really very much a family rite, and second, how making everyone aware of that fact actually increases the effectiveness of the passage. There are other lessons that come forth also. First, the message of the emotional system is a more powerful medium than the cultural tradition, establishing it or perverting it; second, how old traditions, even without articulation of family process, knew about it all the time.

The Jewish tradition of mitzvah (literally, son of [worthy of] the commandments) is fifteen hundred years old, at least. From the religious point of view today, depending on the branch of Judaism, the ceremony can be just the scripture blessing, a reading of the portion in Hebrew, where the child may have just memorized the Hebrew, or a rite with more emphasis on the meaning of the portion, with the child giving more than a stereotyped thank-you speech, adding instead a talk which interprets his portion. But in either case, from the family process point of view, the ceremony always appears to be child-focused.

The first time I began to think of bar mitzvah in family terms was actually before I had trained to do family therapy. I was doing some work as a Community Relations Specialist for the White House. For the first time in my life I began to sense the pressures non-Jews feel around Christmas time. Colleagues I had worked with all year began to become extremely anxious; they began to shop compulsively for gifts beyond their means; drinking became more frequent. Then one Friday evening, as I was leaving a staff Christmas party, on my way to a weekend that was to include a bar mitzvah, things seemed strangely familiar. The anxiety, the gift-giving, the drinking—there was something the two had in common.

Later, when I had the conceptual framework, I began to understand: it was the forces of family togetherness. All the family intensity, the problems with relatives, the unspoken feelings, the pressure to relate, which many individuals spend much of a year trying to avoid, become unavoidable for a Christian near Christmas. For Jewish families, something similar occurs around bar mitzvah. As I began to explore this notion, other events and findings intrigued me. First, a father of a bar mitzvah boy (unbeknownst to me, in line for a transplant) went into heart failure during his son's service, and died. He was an only child, sitting next to his widowed, terribly dependent mother, at the time. This event in turn gained for me an extraordinary amount of additional information. I began to hear an incredible number of reports about other parents cracking up near the time of their son's bar mitzvah, including suicides, breakdowns, and other forms of physical illness. (It is, of course, well known that the suicide rate goes up nationally in late December.)

I began to put things together. No wonder I had never been really successful in calming a bar mitzvah child's anxiety no matter how well prepared he was. It was not his anxiety I was dealing with. No wonder mothers whom I had previously perceived to be models of efficiency and astute reasonableness approached me almost on the verge of hysteria in seeking bar mitzvah dates. No wonder fathers running top government agencies and used to living with daily

crises seemed to go limp at this period. I was dealing with phenomena of far-ranging effects.

Since I knew that a most effective means of dealing with panic
was to offer an alternative mode of behavior, I immediately hit upon
involving the family members more in the ceremony and the preparation. I soon found, both to my surprise and delight, that these efforts had more reward than I expected.

The first change I made was in the method of choosing the portion. Traditionally, there is no choice; one goes by the calendar cycle.
I began to meet with the child, learn a little about him and his family, add what I already knew, and then make several suggestions
based on interest and style, leaving it to child and parents to make
final selections. Then I would have a study session with the entire
family: parents, siblings, grandparents if they were in town, in which
discussion (even argument) was promoted about interpretation. At
the end of the discussion, the child was given the charge that he
would be the teacher for the day. He was told to divide his talk into
three parts: a synopsis in his own words of the portion, his interpretation of what the biblical author was trying to say, and any interpretation he wished to make for today.

After the family meetings I would continue to meet with the bar
or bat child several times to help with the writing of his talk, but I
began to assume less responsibility. Whereas in former days I used
to become terribly concerned about the articulation, coherence, and
overall conceptualization of the talk, I was now primarily concerned
to ask questions (questions which I wanted taken back to the family) that helped with the development of ideas.

Soon, I realized that my role had changed significantly. Instead
of bearing the burden of helping this child through his rite of passage, I had a team to which I was more a coach than the star player.
With that in mind, I also began to make changes in the ceremony.
First, I stopped giving any sermon myself other than an introduc-
tion which described the development of bar mitzvah in Jewish tradition and its further shaping by our congregation. The child was
called as "our teacher for today"; the father, or in some cases both
parents, were asked to bless the child, publicly, out loud or privately.
Since the congregation had a tradition of creative services from the

beginning, families started creating their own services. Continuing with my role as coach, I would make available source books, ask for about six to ten passages, and then take responsibility for fitting them into the prayer order. Families, of course, differed in the extent to which they got into this aspect, some wanting to use standard material which I could select, some becoming so involved that they printed, at their own expense, a supplement which even contained the scripture portion itself in Hebrew and English, and artistic members of the family (sometimes the child himself) began to create designs for the cover. Sometimes a sibling wrote a poem for a frontispiece. One family had a coat-of-arms that went back for generations, and decorated the cover with that.

All families were given the option of having the bar mitzvah at home if they chose. Sometimes musical members of the family played an overture, or background music during the silent prayer. Sometimes a musical child played (on a guitar or trumpet) a tune he created for the service. Since at our services, generally, different portions are read by congregants right from their seats, this procedure was also adopted, as the parents gave out portions of the service to incoming relatives. Blessings over the meal were distributed also, each family being encouraged to give out these responsibilities as seemed natural.

The results have been beyond what I could have foreseen. Family anxiety seems greatly reduced, there is much less focus on materialistic expression, and, despite less direct involvement by me with the child, he generally does a better overall performance. In other words, though I have been trying less hard to "teach" the child myself, whatever process has been released by the transfer in my functioning to the family is also producing more thoughtful, deeper, intellectual efforts on the part of the child.

Finally, though I am less front-and-center, I seem to get even more thanks than before from visiting relatives. The system seems to know.

Funerals, weddings, and the onset of puberty have been universal
rites of passage as long as the human species has had culture. Our
modern culture seems to be producing three other nodal points of
great consequence for the life cycle: divorce, retirement, and geographical uprooting. I should like to devote some words to these
changes as family events also. However, I wish to make clear that I
think there is an important difference between these three and the
former three. The former are all connected to the life cycle biologically. They are part and parcel of being human. It is not as clear to
me that in themselves the latter have the same power for change, unless perhaps they are, as is often the case, residuals of the former
events, e.g., where the divorce or at least the separation came within
a year after an important death, or the geographical move soon after
the marriage. And of course both could be symptomatic of even
larger forces flowing through the family arteries.

These latter also differ in that they are not complete passages,
but more the openings to a passage. With marriage, death, and pubescence, an individual is not simply leaving one state but going to
another, which is well defined. Somehow, the beginning and the
end are all subsumed as part of the complete passage of six months
to a year, and the new state toward which the family is headed is, in
some ways, teleologically pulling the family through the crisis. Similarly, while the biological rites of passage all deal with loss and healing, these latter tend only to deal with loss. They are thus more
open-ended. All of this is not to say they are not ripe times for bringing change to a family, or in some cases symptomatic of changes already going on in the family, but they may not be in themselves
natural family phenomena with all the power for healing that im-
plies.

DIVORCE

The rate of divorce today is becoming so high as to suggest it is reaching the level of a biological imperative, and of these non-biological, nodal points in life, divorce would seem to portend more family change. Several religious groups sensing this have experimented with the creation of a divorce ceremony. (Jewish tradition has had one for fifteen hundred years in which the man hands the bill of divorce to his wife personally, if possible, and says "I divorce you.") Since the thrust of this essay has been that rites of passage are family events, it may be that in many cases only the second marriage or a funeral really completes that passage. Though I do know of one person who sent out divorce announcements with an invitation to a party: "Mrs. . . . announces the divorce of her daughter from Mr. . . . on the steps of the Court House of . . . . " She said that many of her cousins took one look at it and destroyed the card before their husbands could see it.

In order to bring the full power of a family rite of passage to divorce, perhaps the following perspective would be helpful. To the extent a divorce comes about because the rite of passage of marriage did not do its work, which is to successfully bring about disengagement from the family of origin, divorce is also not likely to bring real change if the original triangles are still stuck. To the extent, on the other hand, the divorce is a result of changes in that originally stuck situation with family of origin, which in turn unbalanced the marriage, then the divorce is more likely to offer a new opportunity.

In either case, if clients who come in to work on their fears of loneliness, instability, adjustment of their children, or loss of moorings, which are the focus of most self-help books on divorce, can be focused instead on relationships with their family of origin— and they often are more motivated to do so during this period— one will have made divorce a rite of passage in the fullest sense of the term.

RETIREMENT

Retirement may have more ramifications for family life than has been realized, though therapists who work near military bases don't have to be told this fact. The number of divorces that occur after early military retirement is quite high. The general rule would seem to be this: where the marriage was balanced by mother being intensely involved in the children, and father with the service (which becomes a sort of extended family), his retirement often unbalances the relationship, particularly if he now tries to reenter the family and finds himself excluded, or seeks a replacement in the form of an extramarital relationship. This phenomenon is not limited to the military and can occur with any profession that involves the husband deeply in his work relationship system (lawyers, clergy, etc.). That it has far-reaching ramifications may be seen from the following tale.

A couple, both only children, both twenty-seven, came in to get married after going steady for five years. They had just made the decision and wanted the wedding in a month. Naturally I asked them what they thought moved it on to marriage. Though well educated, introspective, and in no way threatened by the question, they had no idea. Poking around the family history I could find none of the usual family changes such as death, marriage, births. Then innocently she remarked, "Well, the only thing I can say that changed is that both our fathers retired last year." Five years of going steady and they suddenly realized they were right for one another.

One possible explanation of this is that when the fathers retired, they got closer to their wives, who inadvertently let go of their children. Or, maybe this was truer of one who was the real holdout. In any event, theoretically, it is the exact opposite of the former military situation where divorce results when the wife refuses to be drawn closer to the now more available spouse and still clings to the child.

It is thus clear that retirement can have significant family ramifications, and can also be induced by family events—as when a parent, after a loss (through death, divorce, or marriage), begins to wonder, "What's the point of working so hard?" and begins to change his sights. The so-called "leaving the nest" syndrome may be similar. Another major family ramification of retirement is the onset of senile processes. If experience with my mother and aunt have more universal application, the following rule may be true: if around the time any older person begins to reduce their functioning significantly (through retirement or illness), there is available an over-functioning, anxious family member who at that moment has no outlet for his or her energy, the likely outcome is senility for the former.

GEOGRAPHICAL UPROOTING

Geographical uprooting can also have severe consequences, particularly to the extent it means leaving an emotionally important house or community. What is also crucial is the extent to which it changes the balance of a marriage; for example, taking a wife further away from her mother, which can result in her freeing up more or becoming more dependent. In general, it might be said that such uprooting, to the extent it takes a couple further from one spouse's extended family and closer to the other's, will shift the balance, though not necessarily always in the same direction. And I have seen situations where couples move toward a geographical area in which both their extended systems reside almost blow apart in months, despite a previously contented relationship.

From the other side, I have seen more than one family in therapy stuck for months on a marital problem or a problem with a child become suddenly motivated to "resolve things, already" as a deadline nears so that they can get on with their new life.

Here the principle enumerated before is borne out again: families in flux during a rite of passage sometimes can be more easily changed near such moments. It also suggests that the changes which accompany and often precede geographic uprooting or retirement may be much more powerful emotional forces than we realize. And once again, the visible change, that is, the actual retirement or the move, may be symptomatic of emotional changes in the family that had been growing toward a climax for some time.

Our culture, of course, has done little to prepare families for the emotional shock waves of retirement and moves. Though the U.S. government, sensing the life-cycle importance of retirement, in recent years has instituted a program of trial retirement where the person can change his mind during the first year. But even that program may be little more helpful than trial marriage. For it is the homeostatic forces of emotional balance that count and it is very hard to get a true reading on changes in that balance until a commitment is made.

What then about new ceremonies which might help such transitions? It might be possible to create them, but they would have to be centered in the family rather than the work system or the larger community, though, of course, members of those systems would be included.

For here we come face-to-face with what ceremonies are all about. From an individual point of view, a ceremony can help mark a feeling of change or renewal and perhaps make one conscious of a benchmark period in one's life cycle. But it is so much more than that. Ceremonies, even today, get at processes the most ancient tribes were trying to deal with in their most primitive rites. After all, it is only when we think of a person as a member of the family that the word "life cycle" makes any sense. Otherwise we should be talking in terms of "lifelines."

CONCLUSION

I have tried to show that the notion that families are primarily passive vehicles during rites of life passages, with little influence on either the outcome of the passage or the selection of the particular rites and ceremonies, does not hold up. The traditional social science focus on different cultural customs ignores the possibility that the very obvious cultural differences are really rather unimportant themselves. They may be fun to compare, perhaps, but are nowhere near as crucial as the unseen family process forces wearing those very cultural disguises. Indeed, all the cultures of mankind as they become more sophisticated may be participating in a great illusion. Namely, that the "medicine men," for all their hocus pocus, have only succeeded in driving the spooks and spirits further from view, and therefore are harder really to exorcise or control. It is the demons that now wear the masks. There is a great irony here. For the function of ceremonies as rites of passage was originally to keep these very ghosts away from the passage. Now, instead, the cultural disguises they have been enabled to assume allow them to go slipping through, right smack into the next generation.

On the other hand, there is a different ending where members of a family can see through the cultural camouflage and the diversion of the focused individual. When they can maintain their gaze on the family process which contributed to a rite of passage occurring at that particular time, as well as how those processes are at work during the rite of passage itself, that family is in a position to influence both the effectiveness of the passage itself as well as its own emotional system.

Rites of Passage: When the Parents Are No Longer Partners

Friedman noted that this essay "is really about emotional triangles between professionals and clients," which greatly broadens its scope beyond the Jewish bar mitzvah or comparable Christian rites such as confirmation. It was first published as "Bar Mitzva: When the Parents Are No Longer Partners" in Journal of Reform Judaism, *Vol. 28, No. 2 (Spring 1981).*

The increasing rate of divorce among parents is creating a potential fallout of difficulties at the life-cycle ceremonies of their children. While in many cases the divorce has been "friendly" enough to allow the separated or divorced parents to come together and cooperate at the ceremony, often this is not the case. In those situations the conflict, open or not, causes undue complications and stress for the child, the family, and the clergy.

For example, a week before the bar mitzvah of a child of recently divorced parents, the mother, who had remarried during the year, told the natural father that her new husband was insisting on an *aliyah.*[5] The husband responded with, "He was in our bed even

_____

5. Literally "ascent," or "going up," whereby men (and sometimes women) are honored by being called upon to read the Torah aloud to the congregation during the service.

before our marriage ended; if he comes, I won't be there." Two days before the bar mitzvah, the couple brings this problem to the rabbi to solve for them. Because the child had a physical impediment from his early years, he was particularly concerned that this situation not blow up into something that would bring more trauma for the youngster.

How are the clergy to come up with suggestions that are equitable, leave no hard feelings with either parent (which may really mean either side of the family), avoid creating a ricochet effect from the resolution of the immediate problem that would bounce back later in congregational infighting on some "innocent" issue, all the while doing what is best for the child?

Another type of problem when the parents are separated occurs where the mother, having to do everything herself, expects the minister to become the other partner. If the minister accepts this role, given the emotional power of rites of passage, he or she could wind up more a member of that congregant's family than is good for either of them, and this would be equally true whether it is a male functioning as a surrogate husband or a female functioning as a surrogate mother.

This essay is an attempt to describe some of the family emotional dynamics which occur at the time of coming of age ceremonies when the parents are no longer partners. It will also offer suggestions and strategies for dealing with them. Some of the basic principles, however—both about family dynamics as well as the clergyperson's own functioning—will have wider applicability to other nodal events as the life cycle of these same children lengthens.

THE EMOTIONAL SIGNIFICANCE
OF BAR MITZVAH

I have known of more parental dysfunction (from illness, death, and suicide to business problems, separation, and divorce) occurring within the year of this nodal event than at any other significant moment in the Jewish life cycle. My own interest in this phenomenon began fifteen years ago when a father, age forty (unbeknownst to me, in line for a heart transplant), went into massive heart failure during the *amida* of his son's bar mitzvah service and died an hour later. The occasion of a relative fatally collapsing at a personal religious ceremony is extremely rare, so the drama and the singularity of this event forced me to change my focus. As I eventually came to see it, though we tend to say that bar mitzvah is an individual event and confirmation is a group celebration, the opposite is true: confirmation is the individual celebration and bar mitzvah is a family event.

The reasons for the particular emotional intensity of bar mitzvah in a family are complex. I believe one is the heavy investment Jewish parents have in their children, and the extent to which they must face the expectations of their own parents and families both for their children and themselves. Another reason lies in the forces of family togetherness and all the unresolved issues kept at bay over the years through distance. (The bar mitzvah weekend is probably the true basis for the "Encounter Marathon.") Still another factor is an in-law issue. I have noticed that women who were not acceptable to their in-laws often go out of their way to produce a super-achieving child. And, of course, similar dynamics are involved in parent-parent relationships. To the extent any such forces come into play, a mother's anxiety in particular will increase disproportionately to the events of the occasion.

In any event, to the extent I am correct that bar and bat mitzvah is a particularly important moment in the emotional life of Jewish families generally, then it follows that when the parents are separated or divorced, unresolved issues will be particularly prone to surface at this time. And, lest one assume this is more likely to be true at bar rather than bat mitzvah, I should stress that this is not correct. The crucial factor determining the emotional intensity of the occasion is not the sex of the child but the importance of that child to the balance of the parents' marriage, and to the balance of either parent's relationship with his or her own parents.

That actually is the second important variable influencing whether or not any family (but particularly separated or divorced families) will be unusually stressed at this point in the life cycle. To

the extent the bar or bat mitzvah child has particular emotional significance to the marital relationship, or to a parent's relationship
with his or her own parents, the occasion will take on added emotional importance. In any family it could mean a larger turnout, or
a bigger "do," or just more anxiety. Where, however, there are important unresolved issues in the marriage (even after separation and
divorce) or with the grandparents, then when that child "comes of
age," the ensuing stress will produce symptoms wherever the family is vulnerable.

   Depending, then, on the maturity of the parents, a rabbi could
easily find him or herself in the middle of a myriad of "false," that
is, symptomatic, issues having to do with seating, honors, or sudden
illness located in marital, in-law, or ex-spouse relationships. While
some children can rise above all this in their performance, some are
almost done in by it. Here again the variable might depend on the
degree of the child's emotional involvement in the struggle, though
it must be added that I have seen many situations where the conflict,
though present, never surfaces, and this can be even worse for the
child. I once had a situation where the family was known for its
closeness. At the bar mitzvah of their firstborn, the parents wanted
very much to flank their child on either side as he read from the
Torah. In the middle of his portion, he started to faint. The parents
broke up the following year.

THE ROLE OF THE RABBI

A major decision which a rabbi has to make in such situations is to
what extent does he want primarily to keep things calm so that he
can simply do his job on that particular shabbat and to what extent
does he want to take advantage of any emerging crisis to help the
family work through the emotional issues just surfacing. At any life-
cycle event, crisis can be opportunity. This is also true, for example,
before weddings, where conflict with partner or parent is usually
brushed under, thinking that afterward things will get better or not
matter as much: "Let's just get through with it and appease everyone

to do it." In those situations it is definitely shortsighted, since the other side of engagement (to one's partner) is disengagement (from one's family of origin), and there is some evidence to suggest that the strength of the former process is tied to the flexibility in the latter.

With the bar or bat mitzvah, it may also follow that if the issues crystallized by the occasion can be faced, the long-term effect on the child will be healthier than if one just functions for peace. On the other hand, it is not as easy to get the parents to see that, even when one knows them well, or already has them in counseling; and there is some question whether such efforts fall within the province of a rabbi at all.

Even, however, where the rabbi conceives his role to be primarily teacher, efficient or Jewish leader, and has little interest in the "pastoral" aspect of things, there are traps and snares of which it would do every rabbi well to be aware. In addition, the emotional medium always has the power to pervert the values' message. All religious events are just that much more effective when the emotional system of the family is working toward the success of the passage rather than against it.

Using the opening story as a model, I will present an approach that can be helpful to rabbis and families at such intense moments, yet which, ironically, seems to go in the exact opposite direction of being helpful. It is an approach that, on the one hand, avoids the extremes of rushing in, taking over, and getting stuck with the responsibility which rightfully belongs to others, but which also, on the other hand, avoids the opposite extreme of brushing things under the rug in the name of a short-lived peace. At first it might appear to be a cop-out, but actually it can at the same time maximize protection for the rabbi and benefits for the child and family.

THEORY OF AN EMOTIONAL TRIANGLE

There are many ways to conceptualize what is "really" going on in the opening example, and twice as many theories for how to deal with it. A rabbi is at all times involved simultaneously in three different kinds of family systems: his own, his congregation (which functions as a family in its own right), and the families within the congregation (particularly those within his administrative orbit). Not only do these family systems interlock, but problems in one can produce symptoms in another! It seems to me particularly important, therefore, that in all close encounters of the third kind (families within the congregation), the rabbi would do well to keep in mind the other systems also. I will first outline the theory, and then describe how it might be applied to the above model case.

An emotional triangle is formed by any three parts of a work or family relationship system. In a family it can be either three members, or two members and one of their physical or emotional symptoms (affair, smoking, doing badly in school, allergy, heart condition, etc.); in a work system it could be either the congregation, the board, and the rabbi; or the rabbi, his goals, and the congregation; in a counseling situation it could be the rabbi, the couple, and their problem.

There are some specific laws about the way such triangles work that have a very high degree of predictability. For example:

(1) The relationship of any two members of such a triangle is kept in balance by the way a third member relates either to each of them or to their relationship.

(2) It is not possible to change the relationship of the other two directly for more than a week.

(3) Efforts to bring about change in a relationship to which one is not a part, particularly trying to separate them or bring them closer, generally get converted to their opposite intent. As examples, one might consider pushing someone to be more responsible—that is, trying to change a person's relationship to his or her symptom (taking out the garbage, being more punctual)—or pushing someone away from his or her symptom or another person (trying to make someone stop drinking, gambling, or seeing their lover). The effects of such efforts usually blind the other to the dangers in what he or she is doing.

(4) If a person has endeavored unsuccessfully to bring change, the more he or she tries, the more he or she becomes "triangled" into the relationship of the other two. When that occurs—and sometimes it is from the first effort—not only will the efforts be ineffective, if not counter-productive, but also, if the helper becomes too responsible for the problem, he or she will wind up with the stress for the entire system!

(5) Relationship systems have more than one triangle, of course, which often interlock through a common person. For example, a mother could at the same time be in an emotional triangle between her child and her husband, and also between her parents; or also between her child and her mother, or her husband and his mother. Similarly, a rabbi can be in a triangle with two members of a family in the congregation, as well as in a triangle with one of those members (or both) and another individual or family within the administrative system of the congregation. An important feature of interlocking triangles is that to the extent a person is stuck in any one of them, he or she is likely to be stuck in the other(s) also. Conversely, getting "unstuck" in one triangle often will bring more flexibility of action and perception in the other(s).

(6) One "leg" of any emotional triangle tends to be more conflict-ridden than the other two. In "healthier" relationship systems, that conflict will "swing around the horn," so to speak, surfacing in different relationships at different times. In relationship systems with important unworked-out issues, the conflicted or negative side will always be the same, though because of the homeostatic principles enumerated in (1) and (2), that very negativity can keep the triangle in balance (something like Cincinnati retaining its purity by keeping its sin in Covington). The importance of this principle is that members of a relationship system, as much as they may want to see the

negative side change, will also have a vested interest in it not changing.

(7) The way to bring change to the relationship of the other two parts of any triangle (and no one said it would be easy) is to stay in touch with both other parts, without getting caught with the responsibility for their relationship. Anyone can avoid getting caught by distancing, but that just preserves the problem. However, it is equally useless over the long run to stay in touch and get stuck in the middle.

APPLICATION OF THE EMOTIONAL TRIANGLE CONCEPT

In the situation described above, there are at least six important interlocking emotional triangles.

(1) The most obvious does not involve the rabbi at all. It is the woman and her two husbands.

(2) A second is the bar mitzvah child and his two parents (and its precursors, each parent and their parents).

(3) A third is simply the rabbi and the two parents.

(4) A fourth is the rabbi, the parents, and the child.

(5) A fifth is the rabbi, the parents, and their helplessness.

(6) A sixth is the rabbi, his responsibility to the congregation, and the irresponsibility of the family.

With regard to any of these emotional triangles, it is highly probable that to the extent a rabbi allows himself to be caught in the middle, with responsibility for the relationship of the other two parts, he will be ineffective in bringing sound change. Furthermore, it is absolutely predictable that continued efforts to bring change from such a "triangled" position will increase his own stress, with corresponding dangerous potential not just for his health or conflict in his own family. When someone is "noble" or naive enough to take the stress for the system, he loses his capacity to think clearly, see perceptively, and function flexibly.

How, therefore, is a rabbi in such circumstances to help the couple, their families, and the child perpetuate Jewish tradition, and protect himself at the same time? How could he possibly have the Solomonic wisdom to get out unscathed, without either irresponsibly copping out or over-responsibly taking over?

One way might be simply to take direct positions either about what the rabbi is willing to do himself, or to go and support the member of the family whom he thinks is in the right. For example, a rabbi might say, "We have a policy of only direct members of the family," or he might say, "I think this is absurd; I will not permit the other father who is an interloper to have the *aliyah*," or he might support the father by saying, "Your threat to take your ball and go home is childish; it is letting them control the system. Your wife is either just trying to tweak you, or needs you to stand up to her so she can stand up to him." Any of these might keep the rabbi out of the responsible middle, and put the pressure where it belongs.

In many cases, the system of interlocking triangles will be even more complex, perhaps involving the grandparents. Just as importantly, the same immaturity that made this couple come to "Daddy" to solve their problems will keep them helpless or irresponsible in the face of authoritative suggestions or directions.

The approach I wish to suggest may not appear at first to bring results which are definitive, but it can enable the rabbi to deal directly with the emotional processes that brought the couple in to begin with. The rabbi does not have to be an experienced therapist to do it, and when done correctly, in only one meeting it can accomplish long-term results as well. It is based on the above-mentioned notion that if one will allow the triangle to form, and can stay in touch with the two other parts, but without fusing into their relationship, that very stance will modify the intensity of the other relationship. The trick is to stay in touch, but stay unhooked.

Imagine for a moment that two women from your congregation came to you with one child, each claiming she was the true mother.

What King Solomon did in the Bible in suggesting that the child be sawed in half was a masterful "de-triangling" move. Aside from any reverse psychology apparent in the story, he refused to take responsibility. He had the wisdom to know the limits of his wisdom, when not to use his authority. After all, it takes an extraordinary amount of wisdom, intelligence, knowledge, encounters with life, sensitivity, concern, and expertise to know when not to be wise or expert.

A major way of not getting "triangled" but at the same time actually helping a distressed family is in effect to be "helpless" oneself, but again not in some passive, unconcerned way. Rather, one employs approaches that stay in touch but keep the responsibility for the problem where it belongs—in the family. It is remarkable how couples and families will figure out what to do, and work things out in a way that is best—a way that no other human could truly know is best—if the expert to whom the family comes can learn to out-fumble. How? Again, the key is to stay in touch with the process without getting caught in the process.

To begin with, one response I have found to be quite effective is, after listening to both sides, to respond, "Wow, you two really have a problem." And then keep one's mouth shut, no matter how long the silence. (Pushing the other two members of a triangle at one another is a major way of staying unhooked. Here it is a double push-together: the two parents at one another, and the parents at their own problem.) Usually one parent will pick it up from there. The technique at this point is to take whatever one parent says and then ask the other for his or her response, and, after getting that, bouncing it back to the first. The more you can initiate a dialogue between the two, through each talking to you, the more you will reduce their anxiety and change the emotional quality of their relationship. The change in their heads will follow.

A sample dialogue might go as follows:

Father: As I told you, Rabbi, this is all of a sudden. I don't know where she comes off with this idea. Bobby's not his kid.

Rabbi: What is your position on this, Mrs. . . ?

Mother: Bill, my present husband, is part of my family also, Rabbi.

Rabbi: (to father) What would you say to that?

Father: Fine, she can invite him, but giving him an honor is something else.

Rabbi: (to mother) Where do your thoughts go about that distinction?

Mother: I'm not telling him who he can honor. I'm only thinking of Bobby. [snooker #1]

Father: (reacting) Hell you are.

Mother: You're a fine one to talk.

Rabbi: (interrupting in order to modulate the emotional level, to mother) You both seem to have quite a disagreement.

Mother: Bill has been very good to Bobby and I don't want him left out.

Father: Bobby is not his son. Besides, the son-of-a-bitch is an adulterer. He was in my bed with you even before I left the house.

Mother: (reacting) Well, you weren't so innocent either, you know. Throughout our marriage, Rabbi, he's always been quick to recognize faults in others, but not his own. *(Sobs)* What should we do? [snooker #2]

Rabbi: (after pause and with obvious concern) Wow, you two sure have a problem!

Most likely at this point, after some silence, one of the parents would go back to, or bring up, another issue. In that case, the same "de-triangling" by bouncing the issue back and forth should continue, if necessary, until the meeting has to end. Time is on the side of the rabbi if he is in a position to wait them out. If he gets stuck with the responsibility, then the time deadline will increase his own anxiety.

Useful questions that help the "de-triangling" process while staying in touch are: "What would you say to that?" "What is your response" (not "your reaction")? "Where does that send your thoughts?" and other similar neutral phrasings. It also helps if the rabbi does not get too caught up in the content of the issue (and therefore its resolution), but keeps focusing on the triangle and therefore the underlying emotional processes.

If by chance they keep fumbling out, and after the comment that they seem to have a big problem, one says:

> *Parent:* That's why we came to you, Rabbi. You married us [snooker #3], we've never been able to deal with things ourselves. Can't you help (show him/her he's/she's wrong)?

> *Rabbi:* I don't like to admit this, but I feel totally helpless. I just don't know what to say. I care for you both, but this thing's got me stumped. I have been sitting here thinking of what to say to you, but I haven't the slightest idea what would be fair to both of you, help Bobby, and keep your parents calm at the same time. [Added comment on parents is an effort to redirect focus to the emotional triangles where all this probably stems from originally.]

There is nothing wrong with being hopeless as well as helpless. One can say things like, "It seems almost totally unresolvable." Or one can pull a "Solomon." I could imagine the wise king saying, "Well, maybe you ought to call the whole thing off." I have myself done the opposite and suggested that they have two separate bar mitzvahs.

Challenge, of course, is a way of stimulating someone to move without getting stuck with the responsibility for their behavior, or without being seen as taking sides. Perhaps even more Solomonic would be to say to the father: "Listen, you better start doing everything she wants; there's no telling what kind of troubles her husband might stir up in the future."

Again, I wish to emphasize that, for the most part, the very fact that they have come and dumped the problem in the rabbi's lap rather than working it out themselves (as most couples do with most problems) in itself suggests this couple is more stuck or more immature. The ones who are more immature will try harder to get the rabbi to solve the problem for them, which, if he does, will perpetuate the immaturity in the relationship. If the rabbi gets too anxious to solve the problem, well-meaning as the intention may be, and as thoughtful of the child as it is, he supports the basic immaturity in the family.

The emphasis here on finding ways to move the situation without getting caught with the responsibility is thus not just a device designed to protect the rabbi; its aim is to maximize growth and lasting change in the family. Similarly, while suggesting that the bar mitzvah be called off might seem bad for the child, it keeps the rabbi out of one of the most pernicious triangles in our society today (between irresponsible parents and over-responsible others). If he or she can make that suggestion while keeping the parents talking, the pressure they are trying to dump on the rabbi will reverse its flow and force them to take the responsibility. Actually, it would be my guess that suggesting to parents that they call it off, or have two, will do more to get them to think about the welfare of their child than "wisely" telling them to think about the welfare of their child. In fact, if all through this one parent keeps saying, "I am only thinking about our child," that is the one to be wary of. And, again, Solomon is our mentor. His "advice" was not exactly in the best interests of the kid.

The idea of trying to accomplish something by not trying to accomplish it can seem to go not only against our training to be leaders, but also against aspects of our own being that probably selected us for the rabbinical profession to begin with. Staying in touch without getting stuck, however, can be a very powerful method of leading and accomplishing. It converts the trapping dependencies of others in one's favor. And it certainly should not be confused with being non-directive. It is very much taking control. For the techniques described here are designed less to affect the parents directly than to help the helper use his position of authority, and others' inclination to rely on it, as a means of forcing others to take responsibility.

This has been an effort to describe some of the family dynamics occurring at bar mitzvahs or other nodal events and how, through the application of the concept of an emotional triangle, a rabbi can function effectively in the best interests of the family, the child, and himself (his own position). The approaches illustrated here are not the only ones possible, nor is the way of conceptualizing the problem presented here the only way it can be viewed. The emotional triangle concept does seem, however, to have the advantage of giving the rabbi a view that takes into account many aspects of the situation, both within the family and within his own life, that go way beyond the immediate problem. In addition, if our experience in teaching this concept to administrators in government, hospitals, and business organizations is valid, then an understanding of how an emotional triangle operates in any relationship system can allow one to function in the best interest of all (even therapeutically) without the need to "know a lot of psychology." And the reason for that is that it encourages the helper to focus not on the psychology of those seeking help, but on the position of the helper.

The Day God Prayed

This undated sermon on human vanity and hubris must be read in the context of the arms race and nuclear testing in the 1950s and 1960s.

From the Book of Genesis: "These are the generations of Noah. Noah was in his generation a righteous and whole-hearted man; Noah walked with God.... And the earth was corrupt before God, and the earth was filled with violence. And God saw the earth and behold it was corrupt; for all flesh had corrupted their way upon the earth."

And Noah walked with God.

"Noah, Noah, where are you, Noah?" cried his wife. But there was no answer. "Noah, the Fields are here. They are waiting for us. You know the New Year services[6] begin on time."

Still, Noah did not answer. So Noah's wife rushed down to the car and its occupants and began to explain that Noah would surely be right down. When he wasn't, she asked if they had seen him, and when they hadn't, she joined them inside. And after a little while

---

6. Rosh Hashanah, the Jewish New Year and the beginning of the High Holy Days.

they decided he would have to drive himself. "Noah!" his wife yelled one last time, her voice trailing off into the distance.

"Noah!" called out a voice, strong and with authority, yet not without patience, nor lacking in compassion. And Noah turned around. But he saw no one. "Noah," the voice called again, "over here." Noah looked about, but still, he saw no one; yet he was not afraid, only alone. "Why have you not gone to the synagogue with the others?" the voice questioned. "It is the beginning of a new year, Noah; you have never stayed away at this time before."

"I am not sure I can honestly answer that question," replied Noah, slowly, pensive. "You are right, every Rosh Hashanah I have gone without fail to the synagogue. I never questioned why, it just felt right. And this year, too, I didn't question, but then it began not to feel right. And I cannot do what I do not feel is right."

"1 have always liked that quality in you, Noah, but continue— tell me, for you still have not answered why this year you did not feel right."

Noah walked over in the direction from which the voice was coming. He looked about for a place to sit, and finding one, sat down. He did not answer immediately, but closed his eyes and supported his head upon his hands held upward, his elbows on his knees. He rubbed his eyes and stretched, and thought, and looking downward still, began to explain. "It is true that at this time of year, every year, in the past that is, I used to welcome the opportunity to spend a few hours away from all my troubles and worries, and from all the troubles and worries of the world, and thoughts of daily toil. I enjoyed the opportunity to get away from it all. To wrap myself, as it were, in the cloak of the warm notes of the choir, to be stirred, if only ephemerally, by the tones of the cantor, to be inspired, if only for an hour, by the words of the rabbi, and to be uplifted by the passages of the prayer book, promising. . . . "

He paused and pondered, and then continued, gaining speed as if to make up for the lost time. "But this year, as I said, all that just didn't feel right. More than that, it felt kind of eerie, yes, weird. And then I began to ask questions. Why I went in the past. I mean, I never asked to be a Jew. I just accepted it the same way most people accept their religious affiliation, as though it were some part of

me from birth, like a leg or arm. Just a condition. And then I began
to think about all the problems of the world, not Jewish problems,
but human problems, and I began to shudder. All these people starv-
ing, dying, fighting, cheating, lying, running, running, just running
away. I began to feel that—well, I know you may not like this, but
I began to feel that even going to synagogue could be a way of running."

"Or searching, Noah."

"Yes, or searching, but for what? Anyway I began to think. Well,
the world has had many problems before, and things looked mighty
bleak for mankind before. But one could always see past the present to the next decade and hope and reassure oneself and say,
'Things will get better, it'll stop, it'll stop, it'll stop.' But I can't do
that anymore. I can't see into the next decade. It's too far away, and
it's moving too fast, and I only see things getting worse."

He paused a moment and slowed his speech. "You know, I still
might have gone tonight. But then . . . then it was eerie, like a dream.
Maybe I did dream it," he tried to reassure himself. "Maybe I really
heard it."

His voice dropped. "But suddenly, I remembered, me, Noah,
years and years and years ago, when it rained and rained and rained
and my wife kept saying, 'Don't worry, it'll stop, it'll stop.' Well,
you know, I mean, it didn't. It didn't stop, until it was too late. And
of course you came and called and. . . ." Noah hesitated and then
grew pale. He frowned slightly, as though trying to be sure of some
calculation: "And now you've called again," he went on. "Is it to be
again?" he asked.

"Again," the voice answered.

"Is there no hope then?"

"There is always hope, Noah, but there is no evidence."

"But why?" Noah pleaded. "Why? Why now? And what about
the good people? There are many good people. Surely the good will
not be destroyed with the bad, the innocent with the guilty. The
scale surely dips not so heavily downward!"

He began to speak more excitedly, as one possessed with a cause,
yet knowing that it was really himself he was defending. "After all,
for every one who cremates millions, there is one who would save

millions; for every one who sought only to amass millions, there are those who seek to give millions away. For those who manipulate, there are those who respect. For those who are cruel, there are those who are kind; for those who hate, there are those who love; for those who damn, there are those who pity; for those who are apathetic, there are those who are concerned."

Exhausted, he paused, but was quick to resume his plea. "What about all the innocent people who want no part of all the meanness and corruption, who really have had nothing to do with conquests and belligerence, who seek only the happiness of a good and peaceful home, and a job?" Noah's voice softened and stilled. He shook his head slowly and his cheeks glistened a little in the sunset. He raised his head thoughtfully and whispered, "It is not fair. It is not fair."

The voice began to speak again, at first slowly, but always with conviction. "Not all things are fair. Noah. And you are probably correct that there are many good people, but innocent people? No." (The voice growing louder, began to thunder.) "No! There are no innocent people, Noah. Little children and old ladies maybe, but all those 'innocents' who want only a happy home, who want only to be left alone: they mouth answers but they ask no questions. And those who do ask questions turn from their answers lest their consciences cause them to act. In every city of the world, when a child of fifteen or seventeen or twenty murders or steals or destroys, he is guilty, yes, but the others, the victims, they are not innocent. For these murders and thieveries and destruction are backed with all the power of the community unleashed from the chaos of unconcern. In every country of the world, when its leaders plot war and aggression and tyranny, these leaders are guilty, yes, but there are no innocents. Political power is never wrested *from,* Noah, it is always given *to*—by approval or by default. In every part of the world, where corruption, bribery, delusion and injustice are practiced, those who practice it are guilty, Noah, but so are the 'innocents.' They who have winked and blinked their eyes, or closed them on their pillows to wake up each morning as if it were the first day of their lives, they are not innocent, Noah."

"But the rainbow," retorted Noah. "You promised. It was your voice, your words. Never again would all things cease. I know you can answer me with, 'My thoughts are not your thoughts.' But a promise is a promise. You can say we were bad and we released you from your part of the covenant. But you knew we would be bad again—and you promised—the rainbow." Noah had finished. He waited in the silence, and then the voice again began to speak, more calmly this time, almost as though it came forth from the midst of reminiscence.

"Ah, yes," the voice began, "the rainbow. I will have something to say to you about the rainbow a little later, but first, Noah, your question is a good one. Despite all I have spoken, still it is not fair that everything or everyone should be destroyed. And indeed, for quite a while I thought humankind would redeem itself despite the wars, despite the oppression, whether by force or economic or political power, and despite the corruption and dishonesty. I knew what you human beings were, and that your capacity for evil was also your capacity for good. I wanted it that way, so that you might grow and accomplish. I wanted you also to be responsible for yourselves. It is you who make robots, not I. Despite your evil ways, then, I thought you might still redeem yourselves. I never damned you; even that idea was your own.

"In particular, I put my confidence in the descendants of Abraham, Noah. Who more than they expressed my passion for justice and compassion for the afflicted? Who more than they knew how to console and encourage in times of stress, to stir up and agitate in time of complacency? There is no scientific explanation for the prophets, Noah. They and their descendants loved in times of hate, Noah, studied in the midst of ignorance, kept alive ideas of freedom and dignity when others were devouring one another. And when they came to the United States, the nation in whom I had put my confidence, I thought, now, here was a fruitful alliance. For here was the country that would let them live, whose own founding ideas were formed from passions harmonious to their own.

"But something happened, Noah. Something happened to that country. They were all right when it came to developing themselves, but when they had to start being concerned with other countries, they ran away, Noah, they ran away." The voice was quiet, except for a slight murmur. Could it have been a sob? "Everybody started running, Noah, running away from their problems. And they who at times had influenced their country in more responsible directions, they too began to run away—away from their neighbors, away from their problems, away from their identity, away from themselves."

"That's what I mean," said Noah a little bashfully, "when I said that going to synagogue could be a way of running, too."

"Or of searching, as I said before," answered the voice curtly. "But there can be no more running, Noah, no more escaping. The end has come to all running, Noah."

"Then why did you call me?" asked Noah. "You know I would do what I can. What can I do? Build a shelter in an integrated neighborhood perhaps? And get two of every race and two of every. . . . " Noah stopped. "But still," he said, in measured words, "still you continue to avoid the rainbow, the promise not to destroy, even if we are evil, and. . . . "

"All right," the voice cut in. "I will answer your question about the rainbow, though, as you will see, it is painful for me to think about the answer, and I hoped you would get the insight yourself. You had begun to sense so much. But first questions first," the voice sighed. "The shelter is out of the question. It is just another form of running away. Just another way of isolating oneself from the others, another method of being able to avoid crucial questions. In fact," the voice grew louder, "in fact it is just one more example of people deluding themselves, people who have only themselves to blame because they want to be deluded. Noah, do you think it matters how many survive? One hundred or fifty? Or who has more survivors? Why do they not ask what will happen to their way of life, their institutions, their civilization? Once again the same invertedness, the same escape inward to oneself or one's family group. . . . I'm sorry, I just get so angry when I see what human beings have made of themselves. Where were we? Oh yes, the rainbow."

"Yes, the rainbow," Noah echoed firmly, fearfully. "You said you would explain how you could go back on your promise not to destroy the world." There was silence. Noah now had a new fear, that the voice would not speak again and he would be left to wonder how, and why—and then the voice again.

"You have misunderstood, Noah. I will not go back on my promise; the rainbow still is there. I will bring no flood of water or fire or ash or pestilence or blood."

Noah was bewildered. Perhaps he should leave. It was a joke, something to scare him. "Then why all this?" he blurted. "Why have you called me? Why did you say the world would again be destroyed if you are not going back on your promise—and there is much comfort in that—how can the world be chaotic again? Who else will—?"

"Humanity will!" the voice roared. "Humanity has once again corrupted its way upon the earth. My rainbow is still there, Noah, and I see it and I am mindful of it. But humanity is not. They no longer see it; they no longer seek it. They have forsaken beauty and they have made lights so strong and so colorful that they can no longer behold those once beautiful and awesome colors. I have not forgotten my promise, Noah, but they have. They are about to do what I have promised I would never do. Things are not as they were, Noah. That is why there can be no shelter; no shelter, no boat, no plane, no car, no escape—there is no place to go, no escape. There is only confrontation, only action."

"But why didn't you do something? Surely it is not too late. Surely *you* could do something—send some prophet, or...." Noah trembled in the breeze.

"What could be said, Noah, that has not been said? They have heard it so much they do not hear it anymore. And the people that produced the prophets have lost their spontaneity and verve. Prophets? The word all too often rings in their ears with a different meaning. For a while," went on the voice, "I thought I could help, Noah, and I tried. In 1945 there was a new chance. I was overjoyed. It would be a new era. A new day for humanity was dawning, with opportunities never dreamed of. And then they began to come to me and build great buildings, in America and all over. I was encouraged, enthused—but the people were still all answers, no questions. I soon began to realize that it was not always my spirit they sought in these buildings. Still, things might have been all right. But then in 1952, Noah, when that island in the Pacific disappeared...things changed then, Noah."[7] The voice was scolding,

---

7. On November 1, 1952, Americans detonated a hydrogen bomb on Eniwetok Atoll in the Marshall Islands of the central Pacific Ocean.

educating, warning. "I'm not angry," it relented, "just because it was my island. Do not misunderstand. But when I saw what power they had, but no understanding. I'll never forget it, Noah, when I realized what humanity could do.... I prayed...."

"You what?" Noah asked, startled. "You prayed? You?"

"Yes, Noah," the voice went on. "What else could I do? I was helpless. Destroy humankind? There is nothing to it; I could obliterate them in a whiff, as easily as I could conceive of them. But to keep humanity from destroying itself? Ah Noah, this I cannot do—except by reducing them to slaves, robots, merely followers of commands and urges. And then, Noah, don't you see? I would have destroyed them myself. Perhaps it is my fault though. Perhaps I never should have sent Adam east of Eden. At least he would have understood that knowledge is understanding. But I sent him elsewhere. For I wanted him to grow, and he has learned only that knowledge is power."

The voice had hushed, and for a long moment there was only the clatter of crickets and the far-off noise of trains and cars and pots and pans. And then the voice began again. Noah stood transfixed.

"That is why, Noah, there can be no escape. It all depends on you."

"But what can I do?" blurted Noah, perhaps too quickly. "I am only one person." Noah was going to ask more, but felt he might have asked too much already. There was no answer, and Noah knew that he would hear the voice no more.

When Noah returned home, his wife and friends were already lounging in the living room. At first, they didn't even notice him as he entered, and then, all at once, he was the center of their attention.

"Well, here you are!"

"Where were you?"

"We wondered what happened to you."

"Frankly, I was beginning to worry."

"You missed a beautiful service, Noah—a great sermon, too!"

Noah paused a moment, looked at them, and headed for the stairs.

"Hey, Noah, where are you going? You still haven't told us where you've been. Happy New Year, Noah! *Shana tovah!*"

"Oh. Happy New Year," Noah returned. "It is a new year, isn't it? I wonder if it really will be new?" Noah thought aloud.

"What's that?" someone began to ask.

"Excuse me for being a poor host," Noah continued, "but I'm very tired. Good night, everybody."

"So early?" His wife was astonished.

"Yes," Noah answered, "I want to get an early start the first morning. There is—that is—" Noah corrected himself, "I have so much work to do."

"But you still haven't told us where you were," a guest called out.

"Oh!" Noah uttered. "I went for a walk," he said, blandly. "Yes," he said, "I went for a walk with . . . I just walked."

These are the generations of Noah. Noah was in his generation a righteous and wholehearted man, and the earth was corrupt before God. And the earth was filled with violence, for all flesh had corrupted their way upon the earth. And Noah walked with God.

An Interview with God

Rosh Hashanah, September 13, 1977,
Bethesda Jewish Congregation

Being the transcript of a cassette mysteriously found in the crags of the rocky coast of Maine in the summer of 1977.

Reporter: First of all, on behalf of all my colleagues I want to thank you for the honor of granting this interview. I must be the first since Moses to be allowed into your presence.

God: You're quite welcome. Actually, there have been a few others over the years but they spent all their time trying to butter me up or change me, or analyze me, or they misunderstood me so badly that when they went to publish what I said, I could not permit it. A few tried anyway so I just made sure everyone thought they were crazy. In all events, you understand the rules.

Reporter: Yes, I think so. I may ask any question that leads to more understanding of life, that is, the human condition, but I may not ask anything about the future or get personal.

God: That is correct. Please begin.

Reporter: Well, I guess the first question that most people would want to know is what's it all about? I mean, why are we here, that sort of thing.

107

God: Here we go again with my inscrutable will.

Reporter: I guess you could call it that. After all, every generation for the past several thousand years has produced someone who tried to explain it. Even when it became popular to say you were, pardon the expression, "dead," others were saying that's exactly what you wanted them to think. But I don't really intend the question to be that abstract. For the average person existence is quite frightening, at the least, and often, quite a bore. It's hard to imagine that, given the grandeur of your whole creation at its most majestic, you are content with the banality of the average life. Yet it's hard to see how it might fit in with your divine plans.

God: Then let me get something straight immediately. I realize it has gotten around down there that I have some extraordinary plan toward which everything is inexorably headed. But it's just not so. In fact, one of the reasons I said that you may not ask questions about the future is that I'm really not always sure myself how things will turn out.

Reporter: But you're supposed to be a God who *cares*. No matter how differently human beings have tried to interpret your will, all agree you are a God who cares. I mean, even the deists who say you left after you created a perfect world assume it was a beneficent world. We are, after all, your creatures.

God: Did you have to remind me of that? That's all I hear. Oh, the dependency of it all! Why, would you believe that one of my ministering angels recently did some tabulating of the supplications I have received over the last century or so and found that in 90 percent of the petitions sent here from earth, the person praying reminded me that I was his creator?

Reporter: You mean that isn't true either?

God: No, I mean, yes. In a manner of speaking, it's true. But what does that have to do with it? You're a parent, aren't you?

Reporter: Yes.

God: How would you like it if every time one of your children wanted something, he reminded you that you and your wife had created him?

Reporter: I see what you mean.

God: The issue of whether or not I care has nothing to do with my being the creator. The only alternative to complete control is not capriciousness. Of course I care what happens to my creatures. It's my image, isn't it? But the notion that I concern myself with each one's everyday existence—what a conceit—it's only found among earthlings and, I might add, misses the whole point of creation.

Reporter: I think I'm beginning to understand. If there are other stars with other planets, and other galaxies with other stars—you just wouldn't have the time.

God: It's not a matter of time. It's a matter of focus.

Reporter: Then maybe I don't understand.

God: Nor do most of your species. Life is viewed by the average human being as something static, as though there were some hidden structure, some basic reality inside their head or out that, once discovered, would reveal all the answers.

Reporter: What a shock this is going to be to the intellectuals.

God: They just represent one of the extremes. Most people don't do any searching at all, but they're often as well off as those who devote their whole life to searching.

Reporter: You mean people need time to relax, have fun. If the un-examined life isn't worth living, neither is the over-examined one.

God: Not quite. Let me go on. It's not the amount of searching that counts, but the nature of the searching attitude. Take, for example, someone who has to make a major decision about the future, per-haps getting married, a job, deciding where to live. It's true that many do not plan enough, but many others worry incessantly about what is right, almost to the point of immobilization. The main point, however, is this: both groups focus on the problem from the point of view of making the right decision. If things turn out well, they will say, "I made a good decision." If not, it was the wrong de-cision. It's as though the whole situation was preordained and what they do is find out the hidden reality—supposedly already in existence in space and time, waiting for them.

Reporter: Wait a minute. Let me understand this. If life is not out there simply to be discovered, then it must be a process rather than a state of being.

God: Exactly. I am not saying, of course, that there is no reality, that the world merely exists in my mind or, for that matter, merely in the mind of anyone else. But rather, knowing reality is not enough. It's only part of the truth. And this, you see, is where *focus* comes in. The key to knowledge is perception, and perception is in turn a matter of focus. Now we can go back to the matter of my concern for my creatures. It is true that I used to be more concerned. I focused on everything that took place everywhere. But I found there was a declining return on that effort. The concern helped to a point, and then it was as though a threshold was reached. Soon it was not very fruitful, and eventually it even became harmful.

Reporter: You mean you got overprotective?

God: No, I mean something much deeper than that. I mean I lost my objectivity. And that had two ramifications. The smaller and more immediate one was that I couldn't always discern what was best for any given creature at any given time. I was too involved.

Reporter: And I imagine it became difficult to make sure that in helping one you weren't hurting another.

God: Oh, no. That's easy, anything that can be reduced to quantifying I can handle. After all, my mind is generations beyond your most advanced computers. But there are some phenomena of existence that are not quantifiable, not because of their complexity, but because they just don't lend themselves to that sort of thing. And one of those phenomena is focus. The real problem with caring so much was that I began to give so much attention to everyone and everything that I lost my perspective on where I was headed. I forgot about my own growth.

Reporter: That must have been around the Middle Ages, say, just before the Renaissance. But how were you able to change this?

God: You're close. Actually it was a little earlier than that. But speaking of the Middle Ages, there was one group that at precisely that time caught on to what I had done. Have you ever heard of the Kabbalah? They were an esoteric group of Jews, I believe, filled with all sorts of mystical notions and magical rites. But they were also searchers, and sometimes precisely because they had given up on the supremacy of reason and recognized the irrationality of always being rational that they developed a concept which they called the *tzimtzum.* The word means to "contract" or "shrivel up." If I am able to contract myself, it explains why a beneficent creator can co-exist with evil in the same world. They had guessed correctly, if for the wrong reason, that I had contracted myself, which, by the way, is not to be confused with withdrawal.

Reporter: Again, let me try to understand this correctly. After all, I am going to have to explain it to my readers. Basically you withdrew—excuse me, you *contracted* yourself—so that you could be more concerned with your larger purposes.

God: Correct, or at least that's part of it. I could always come back in now and then if I thought it was absolutely necessary.

Reporter: I'm beginning to see, and part of the cost was permitting evil, suffering, and tragedy.

God: Well, that's a typical earthling's way of looking at it. What I found was that the good which was achieved while I was not omnipresent was much more enduring and of a much richer quality. That's really why I continued the *tzimtzum.*

Reporter: Wow, speaking of perspective, that sure is a different way of looking at good and evil. On earth we always tend to relate them, see them as opposing forces, or as by-products of the same source such as our free will. Almost all our thinkers who have dealt with the subject, whether from the point of view of religion, politics, or philosophy, tend to see good and evil as adversaries. But you're saying something way beyond that. You seem to be saying that by allowing for evil one makes possible a still greater good. That sure is a change in focus.

God: You're getting it. I am not saying that evil can be ignored. Nor am I saying that simply focusing on the good is enough, not at all. But if one only focuses on the elimination of evil then it becomes difficult to see how whatever has been labeled good can also be destructive.

Reporter: I'm afraid you've lost me again.

God: Well, you know the issue of good and evil is at the very heart of existence. Not only on earth but throughout the universe. In fact it is the constant preoccupation of the heavenly host. You have no idea how obsessed my ministering angels are with the problem. And when Satan comes by and taunts them about being totalitarian goodnicks. . . .

Reporter: Excuse me? Satan comes up here?

God: Of course, he's one of my favorites. Oh, yes, all that stuff about him being a fiend doing horrible things, fallen angel—well, it's true. He is quite a devil. But actually he just likes to take the other side. Frankly, he's the only one I can really talk to. In all events, whenever the heavenly host congregates to discuss what is best for humanity, Satan helps keep things in perspective. Actually the mere sight of him drives the others up the wall. He keeps telling them that their ideas come out of what they think is best for them, not really what is best for human beings. They think he's just trying to trick them when he says things like that. They're always very straight, you know.

Reporter: This is really interesting. Could you give me an example?

God: Sure, take the problem of natural resources everyone is now so worried about down in your country. The angels are all on the side of conservation, of course. They've been scurrying around everywhere giving people ideas about how to save fuel, make better engines, smaller cars, reminding people about their responsibilities to future generations. Their biggest thing was the fifty-five-mile-an-hour speed limit. Remember those three men who drove from the Midwest three abreast at fifty-five miles per hour and preventing any cars from passing them for a thousand miles? That was direct inspiration from one of my purest. Well, Satan hears about this and he really gave them hell, so to speak. He told them that all they were doing was making it easier for the politicians and the oil companies. He arrived with all kinds of tables he'd worked out to show that what they were doing was driving the cost higher by making people conserve. Instead, we should go right on using the oil freely, thus keeping the price down, and using the money saved that way to find new forms of energy instead of putting it into the pockets of the oil companies and, through taxes, the politicians.

Reporter: That's a different way of looking at it. But doesn't he realize that people might not give that money up so easily if they had to do it voluntarily? It seems to me the angels have a much more realistic view of things.

God: Well, that's, of course, one of the biggest differences between them. The angels are always on the side of protecting people from their weaknesses. Whereas Satan, in a way, has more faith in my creatures. He'd rather save them by challenging them, creating crises on purpose, let things rise to their natural level. I guess that's why he's often seen as encouraging evil.

Reporter: But what about saving life? I mean, what would he say about those statistics that show that a reduced speed limit is saving lives?

God: He loves that one. First he suggests to the angels that if it is true, then why don't they reduce it to fifty or even forty, and adds, "Think of how many lives that would save." He's very consistent, you see. Even there, he is willing to let evil or tragedy come as long as people are being encouraged to go higher. Actually, if it were up to him, he'd take the speed limits off altogether—not to encourage licentiousness, but to get rid of the speeders. His idea is that if you allowed everyone to go at their own rate, there would be an evolutionary effect and the irresponsible ones would just kill themselves off.

Reporter: Taking a few of the responsible ones with them.

God: That's exactly what the angels tell him. But he's no fool. He comes right back, showing that it would keep the good guys more responsible also by giving them less excuse to blame their misfortunes on the bad guys.

Reporter: That almost sounds like a kind of no-fault ethics.

God: You should hear him on no-fault marriage instead of no-fault divorce. Another of his favorite themes is how saintliness causes guilt. He also wants to give parents workshops in insensitivity training. What seems to bug him most is when he sees people or causes or ideas described as "good" when the fact of the matter is that the people who act that way are not doing it out of choice but because they can't help being any other way to begin with. For him those three motorists who drove three abreast from the Midwest weren't on the side of good, but simply on the side of themselves. He sees the whole conservation thing as an obstructionist's dream. In fact he told the angels that in inspiring those three to do that, they had just allowed them to nationalize their neuroses.

Reporter: He really is a devil.

God: But he does help keep things in focus. Of course, it's possible to get too caught up in this conservation issue, it's just an example. The important principle is that Satan is a little more adventurous than the angels. It's true he tends to see them as controlling, using terms like good, reasonable, or sound economy as red herrings that disguise the fact that they're just trying to impose their own will. What I like about him, though, is that he keeps the angels on their toes. He helps provide a balanced perspective which, as we have been saying, is essential to keeping focus flexible. And, I guess, it would have to be said that he's a little more predisposed toward the continued evolution of man.

Reporter: You're on the side of evolution? Wait till some people I know hear that!

God: But surely it follows from everything else I've said.

Reporter: Yes, but to think that the author of Genesis got it so wrong. It means one of the major works interpreting your will is misleading.

God: But Genesis has it right—it's the interpretations which mislead. I mean, there are some mistakes in Genesis, of course. For example, you don't think we really suddenly stopped that Tower of Babel thing because we were threatened? Or take the flood, for example. The real reason I had to stop the rain was because the ark began to leak. Noah sure was righteous, but when it came to ship building—yechhh! He was a terrible, sloppy craftsman. On the important issues, however, such as what is human, there Genesis has it right. Human beings are animals and yet they're not; they're different and yet they're the same. They came last and yet came first. They were made all at once, and yet they aren't finished. Their brain differentiates them, and yet it doesn't.

Reporter: Wait a minute! You're going too fast. I follow you up to that last point. If you take Genesis metaphorically, then I see it, but what do you mean that the human brain is more advanced and yet it isn't?

God: Well, as some of your scientists are just beginning to find out, the inner core of the brain or what you call the limbic system—the seat of your emotions—has not gone through the same evolutionary processes as the rest of your cerebral physiology. It is exactly the same as in the other higher forms of mammalian life.

Reporter: So that when we let that part of us rule ourselves, we are just like any other organism, responding on a pleasure-pain principle alone?

God: It's a little worse than that. Because you are actually capable of complex thought and speech patterns, when you let your limbic system take over, the cerebration which accompanies it may appear to be thinking, but it isn't. When that happens, your thoughts are no longer the clue to what motivates you, but symptoms of emotional positions.

Reporter: I can see that would explain a lot of the reactions, interchanges, and the lack of communication between people. But it does seem to me that maybe you ought to go back to the drawing board, so to speak. You'll pardon me for asking this, but don't you think whoever had charge of that design which kept the limbic system from evolving further botched the job?

God: But this wasn't our first try. The rabbis even mention that in their midrash. They were right. We tried a world first that was all full of feeling, compassion, and love, but no one could stand up to their destructive impulses and eventually they just ate one another up, the innocent going first. Then we tried it the other way; created a world of perfect intellects with an absolute sense of right and justice.

Reporter: What happened there?

God: Again the rabbis had it right. Without any feelings to balance the intellect, that world was also destroyed by harshness. The rabbis guessed correctly that some combination was the next choice, but they failed to discern the real reason that this intellectual world didn't work. One of the things we had tried was read-outs in everyone's foreheads so that everyone could know exactly what everyone else was thinking by just looking at them. We figured that would do away with all dissembling and cheating. Perfect communication was what we envisioned.

Reporter: So what went wrong?

God: One day the creatures saw their reflections in a mirror and all of them became so obsessed with reading their own minds that they just stopped relating to anyone else.

Reporter: So human beings, as we are, really are a compromise.

God: I don't see it that way. For while you do have as much capacity for feeling or intellect as before, whenever you can keep yourselves from going to one extreme, each attribute helps inform the other and thus produces richer and deeper results than if only one had been used exclusively.

Reporter: And I can see the combination helps us to maintain focus, to use your word.

God: Correct. You see if we call human beings a compromise between the extremes of the feeling animal world on the one hand, and the god-like intellect on the other, then it makes it sound as though there is some midpoint on that continuum which is just right. But the key is not finding the right mixture, it is being able to change the mixture in response to the challenges of life; and that is where a broader focus is essential.

Reporter: This is not going to be taken well by all those salvation-ists—religious, political, and psychotherapeutic—who think they have found the right formula.

God: Yes, the salvationistic impulse is almost inherently antithetical to evolution because it thinks in binary terms, saved and lost. The human cell is binary—on and off—but you do not have to be that way. This is really what differentiates you from the lower forms of life, biologically and existentially. The key to your continued evo-lution is to follow the same path you have trod thus far. You have come a long way from a single cell and you no longer need to think, feel, or relate only in binary terms. Whenever you do that, no mat-ter how sophisticated your behavior or ideas seem at the moment, you regress to the most primitive level of your biological ancestors.

Reporter: I guess I never thought of God as primarily a biologist.

God: Listen, Crick and Watson got their Nobel only for describing the shape of DNA. I, after all, invented it, and as you can see, not without considerable experiment and consideration.

Reporter: Well, I know my appointed time is running out. Let me, if you would, try to summarize so I'm sure I got it straight. And I do have one more question. I came here primarily to understand your will. I thought that's what most people would be interested in. But somehow we keep going back to human identity as the key issue. As I understand the essence of everything you have said, the key to our future is not some specific goal or purpose structured into the nature of life, but rather how we manage our assets.

God: Exactly! That's why I have emphasized becoming and chal-lenge. Human beings tend to focus on me. Since I did the *tzimtzum* I had hoped you would be better able to focus on yourselves. Many of you have, but many more still keep trying to understand and de-fine me or their leaders instead of yourselves. However, you said you had one more question. Go ahead.

Reporter: It has something to do with what you just said. We have been talking about individuals, and yet people are people. They want to and almost need to relate to one another. Don't you think relationships are important in developing an identity?

God: Absolutely. I'm surprised you ask. In a way I thought that's what we had really been talking about all the time. The relationship between any two individuals is the most powerful force in creation for retarding human evolution. I saw that when I created Eve, of course, but it became all the more apparent to me after the *tzimtzum.* For the truth of the matter is, and this is off the record, that one of the reasons I had to contract myself is that they were beginning to devour *me.* It was partly self-preservation. Then, when I stopped being so involved and concerned all the time to help or set limits, and began to focus instead on my own growth, I found that in the process I was automatically setting limits to how much I would let them invade my space. And many responded with leaps in their own growth as well. Human evolution is through your relationships with one another, particularly your ability to tolerate evolution in the other. Growth is natural. The key is, on the one hand, knowing how to stay out of its way, and on the other hand, not letting the growth of another take over your existential DNA.

Reporter: That almost sounds more like virology than ethics.

God: They are very close. You may tell your readers that the identity of any piece of protoplasm can be destroyed or enhanced by the functioning of the organism closest to it . . . if you let it.

Reporter: Well, I'm not sure I will publish this. It's not quite what I expected. I mean, I appreciate your time and it's been a wonderful experience, but as for my readers, I'm afraid they just would never believe me. They would probably dismiss me as some kook.

God: I don't know why you say that. After all, you won't be the first to have claimed to have heard my voice. Not at all.

Reporter: Oh, no. It's not that. As far as telling people that the interview took place, no trouble there. It would probably be quite easy to get millions to believe *that.* It's what you actually said—your answers, your ideas, what you really stand for. How on earth could I ever get them to believe that?

Part Three

ACCEPTING
MORTALITY

"I Shall Not Go Gently into that Good Night"

Diary from October through November, 1980

* In October 1980, at the age of forty-eight, Edwin Friedman was diagnosed with major arterial blockage and required immediate quadruple bypass surgery. In *A Failure of Nerve,* he later discussed the ways this surgery and recovery gave him the opportunity to work on himself and his family relationships; these diary entries provide an "eyewitness account" of his diagnosis, surgery, and recovery during the months of October and November. This experience motivated Friedman to apply his own theories to himself and also provided new channels of communication to help him in the healing process. He had always believed that the most useful way to coach another human being was for the supervisor, mentor, teacher, or therapist to work on his or her own differentiation of self. In fact, Friedman believed that someone could not move or develop beyond the degree to which the helping professional *had* worked on self-differentiation. These entries provide the opportunity to see more clearly how he lived this belief.

DIAGNOSIS

I can't believe it. Angina, me! The pains have not been in the chest. I still think it's a GI problem, but the treatment only worked for a few days and they did say there was a change in the cardiogram. The cardiologist is too sure of himself, and yet the thing has gotten worse over the past year. Still, I had the same pains in April and the cardiogram was OK then. Imagine, me walking around with Nitro and he says keep it with me at all times, "upstairs and down, driving or walking." Shades of my father and at almost the exact same age, too. Good God, is there really a kind of built-in obsolescence in people? Suppose I need a bypass? That's for other people—I've always known how to handle stress. Geez, I've been under a lot the last few years, the death of my mother, leaving the congregation, and more. But I thought I was handling it well. Could my notions of stress be that wrong? Still, I can't believe it's the genetic alone, genetics just don't work that way; there have to be other factors also. Cholesterol? Years ago, yes, but I've cut back so much.

Boy, did I get anxious when the cardiologist pronounced the sentence. I wanted him to forgive me and take it away. No wonder the ancient kings killed the messengers that brought them the bad news! Still, the verdict isn't in yet. Tomorrow the halter, Friday the stress test. And I'm just at the peak of my form, damn it, everything just about to break for me. (What a double entendre that is.) Oh well, I've always been a survivor. And yet, maybe all these approaches to taking charge of one's life, and making decisions are illusions. Suppose even decisions are illusions. Maybe we only think they matter. And I thought I was handling my life well.

A meeting with the publishers, speaking engagements all over—now I have to cancel a whole workshop for Friday for this damn stress test! I never have problems when I am speaking—performing—the cardiologist is too anxious to make a diagnosis. I have to watch that one, he doesn't understand the emotional component. I'm never more relaxed than when I'm performing. But I did almost miss two planes last week. I can only walk thirty feet carrying something and then have to rest for almost five minutes. I have adapted to this thing far more than I realized.

Now I'm having more symptoms since the diagnosis. Is that possible? That's ridiculous. Am I more aware of them? I must guard against the self-fulfilling qualities of diagnosis, the dependency on authority to determine my view of me. That's what my father did; he got caught in the medical inevitability. This halter is really something—I feel like a robot, someone out there is monitoring me. Write down every significant pain or emotional upset so they can correlate the time to the heartbeat. That's what a novel really is, isn't it! I'm going to give them the best twenty-four-hour record of one man's existence since Joyce wrote *Ulysses*! I still don't think I should have cancelled that workshop. It's not just the money; it's the whole idea of losing momentum. I'm scared shitless.

Three and a half minutes, and you're supposed to last eight to twelve! Now an angiogram. I've read about those things. They actually put it in your heart—I think I'm more scared about their going up through the groin. Isn't medicine wonderful. The doctor's good, but look at my hostility—kill the messenger—he said now he wasn't sorry he asked me to cancel the workshop. How the hell am I ever going to decide when to follow a doctor's order and when to reserve my own judgment. That's going to be a big issue throughout. "Ninety-five percent chance of a bypass," said one, the other said, "Let's see." But he's the one who insisted on the test. How could this have all happened so suddenly! There were no symptoms. Or at least what there was, wasn't in the chest. Except that one night a couple of weeks ago. I must have really been close. What pain—felt it in my elbows, trouble breathing, but more like in the stomach, sweating, nausea. I must have stood still for twenty minutes, maybe even a half-hour, just leaning against the wall. I should have known then. If Type A's have more heart attacks, maybe it's because we try to push through the symptoms in our desire to achieve our goals rather than because our aggressiveness in some ways hurts our heart.

I feel so lonely. No one can help me now. I will have to start checking things out with my family. I really don't think anyone else had angina except my father. His brother died of cancer. Oh yes, one of my mother's brothers had angina, but he died at eighty-nine. And none of my cousins on either side—and they are almost all male—show any kind of heart problems. I still can't believe this is happening.

Started calling friends and family. Wow, have they been supportive. They also are surprised, so I must have been putting on one hell of an act. Have to admit to feeling good when they get anxious. Is it that I just enjoy shocking people, getting attention? It's also spreading the burden, the risk. How shall I explain all my somaticizing over the years: slipped disc as teenager, appendectomy at eight, maybe polio in my twenties, allergies, two hernias, gout in more recent years, Achilles tendon ripped twenty-one years ago, all those twisted and broken ankles playing ball as a kid, even a broken arm. I've always just taken them for granted because I heal so fast. But this one is different. This suggests something chronic rather than acute, something that has been going on for a longer time than I care to admit. Yet I have never seen myself as a sickly person. These things just come on every now and then—and always so unexpectedly.

Saw a client today with a similar history now going in for serious surgery (as compared to playful surgery?) and I asked him if he saw his body as his friend. The question blew his mind. His lower bowel keeps bleeding after he gets upset, so they do a temporary colostomy, it's no longer connected up, and it still bleeds when he get upset. Can emotions be located in parts of the body?

If my symptoms could talk, what would they say to me? That's what a former client told me I asked *him* when he was having a lot of physical problems. My answer was (to myself—and it was almost automatic), you take care of us and we'll take care of you. I do not think I have seen my body as my friend. If so, I have used my friend, maybe even abused it. It's the old body and soul thing. Your body isn't to be equated with your self, and yet without it you ain't got no way of being—without it you can't be defined apart from others. If they ever get around to doing head transplanting, what will they really be transplanting, the head or the body? I mean, whose name would go with which part?

What support I'm getting, even from relatives whom I thought were angry at me. What a good feeling! I'm calling them to create a relationship system, of course, to avoid the isolation, and yet I can't just say I'm scared or I need your help. I never thought I would be the first in my generation to die. But maybe I won't even need the operation. I haven't even taken the angiogram yet—and look at me, already doing research on surgeons. Again the support has been unbelievable. Two friends who don't even know each other showed up with the same statistics: there is a definite correlation between the number of procedures a team does and their mortality rate. Two stand out in Washington, but Cleveland and Houston are better. Still, one here was trained in Cleveland and he seems to be the one the doctors go to themselves. When you find a lot of Italians in an Italian restaurant, you know that's the place to go. The eat-where-the-trailer-trucks-are-parked philosophy.

My worries really have been about what happens beyond the operation; if this could happen once, why not again? Some are suggesting biofeedback, but I've always found that so kooky.[8] Yet I must get control. I do believe that's possible—my whole life has been based on that principle of not being a victim, seeking ways to be the master of one's fate, one's own boss. But suppose Someone Else is pulling the strings?

---

8. Friedman later became an advocate of biofeedback and applied it to himself after other surgeries.

And yet there is evidence of people getting control. What is so intriguing is that what seems to be peculiar to heart conditions also shows up with regard to the GI tract (ulcers, colitis, etc.) and the bronchial system (asthma). All three biological systems are smooth muscle systems, what they used to call the involuntary responses. I sure had better do something to make them more voluntary! I like the idea of "buying time" also. It gives me a strategy and a way of prioritizing my hours and thoughts and concerns. This has been an important day. I again have hope, not because of the surgeon's skill, but because something is left in my hands for after, and forever.

Today I began making decisions. It is clear that a life-threatening illness is like a rite of passage, and the operation is the ceremony. I'm supposed to be the expert on a family approach to rites of passage, so I had better start involving my family in this operation as I've advised others to involve their families at the time of weddings, funerals, and bar mitzvahs. I've got to include them even more. Even now I can see that this passage is going to affect everyone's relationship with me; they're all going through the passage, too. There is another parallel. If I have written that the marriage begins before the wedding, and the funeral before the death, then it follows that recuperation begins before the operation! Also I think I have figured out how to deal with the doctors, how to take advantage of their knowledge and expertise (even if they conflict) and still not get caught in medical inevitability. (Every time they say "coronary artery disease" I want to correct them and say, "Not disease, dysfunction.")

The model I came up with must have been influenced by the upcoming election, and my knowledge of politics. They're advisors, damn it, not auto mechanics, and I shall treat them as a president would his advisors and assume they know far more than I in their various fields of expertise. I must go to them for a knowledge-base, but like any good president, I'll be damned if I'll let them make policy! I have to make the decisions because I was the one elected. They were simply *selected*—by me. Only I have to answer to myself. I must not give them that responsibility, no less resign. And only I have the overall perspective to make judgments.

Tomorrow, the hospital. It may be my first of several stays. I have to remember that physicians respond to the anxiety of the patient, one way or another. They either get too sympathetic and lose their objectivity, or too rigid and lose their humanity. They're only human. I learned that in dealing with my mother's doctors. The big question is, what can I do to stay loose, which in turn will help everyone else stay loose? I don't want over-diagnosing or misman-agement. I'm sure humor will help and I guess just trying to be clin-ical. Taking a research, scientific approach, and keeping my anxiety to myself. But institutions scare me.

I have always assumed that the major factor in stress is staying out of triangles, out of the middle. That as long as you are doing it for yourself, you can handle an almost incalculable amount of stress, but when you get caught trying to work out someone else's prob-lems—your kids', your spouse's, your parents', even your grandpar-ents' (even after they are dead if you got stuck with the right message)—that's when you get done in. And maybe these new ideas I'm hearing about are not incompatible. But they sure add a broader dimension. One is that little paper on biofeedback. He is saying that everyone somaticizes in their own idiosyncratic way. When the system gets stressed it will come back to normal, but go over a cer-tain range and the whole thing goes out of balance, and may not be rebalanced except by extraordinary measures. Then there's the no-tion of maximum limitations. It may be that a person has just so much stress-reserve, like a woman's ovaries—they never get replen-ished, but start with their full complement from the beginning. As we use up that reserve, we don't get that kind of strength back. It's only a model, of course, but it sure makes sense. By God, I went into the fiery furnace these past few years and it's a wonder I have any strength left at all. I must be basically far more healthy than I thought. I think also I was counter-phobic, a "counter-coward"—I never ran from a challenge. That is going to have to stop. Clearly the

major thing I'm going to have to do after this is all over is reorder
my priorities, and in a way that I can define, or at least be more cir-
cumspect about those I choose to rise against. Tomorrow the angiogram, next week the world.

That angiogram was something. Why is it that little things inside
the body always seem so much bigger than they really are? A pim-
ple in the ear, a sore in the mouth, and now we can add to that a
fishhook in your heart. It all seemed so routine, and they said they
did it in record time. Of course they did—they didn't even have to
bother with one of the arteries, it's 100 percent closed. What terrible results. My left main is 99 percent closed, in addition, and the
circumflex is two-thirds gone. I've been walking a tightrope for
months. I've been on the precipice and never knew it, like walking
blindfolded along the edge of a cliff and not knowing the cliff was
there, and all the time thinking I was on solid ground. Still, I'm
lucky as the devil. But how could it have come on like this with so
little warning?

But back to the truly frightening present: the map shows multiple occlusions all over the arteries and in the collateral system as
well, maybe thirteen or fourteen. It looks like cancer, multiple
melanoma. It is disease and not dysfunction; it's rampant, out of
control. Is it really possible to come back from this? Not just from
an operation, but from practically starting over? That picture says
something has been awfully, no, totally, yes totally wrong, either in
my behavior or in my body, and can one make a significant change
about something that total?

These have been the two most efficient weeks of my life (and maybe
the last). It's absolutely amazing what deadlines do for you. I have
been able all at the same time to do one round of my practice,
phone all those people, write a few letters, and organize my finances
into three plans for the family: one if I die, one if I don't die but

become a vegetable, and one if I survive but can't bring in income for a while. And I have been able to think so clearly about all these plans. Meantime, though, I can't help thinking about my father's condition at almost the same age, but especially when he died, seven years later. He and I never talked about it. I, on the other hand, took each of my kids, sat them down and told them what they must be prepared for and what I thought of them. How much I loved them and what good qualities I thought they possessed. Each was really surprisingly impassive. It made me feel good to do it, though. Everyone should do it every day so they don't think of it too late, as the plane is going down. Those years of my father's decline were like a huge rehearsal. The ironies of history. What if they had had this procedure then? Actually the angiogram was invented shortly after he died. And what procedure will they invent shortly after I die, whether it is now or a quarter-century from now? And him sitting there, eating his daily eggs, which he always fried in butter.

My friend Florence is right. I've been going around automatically saying, "And my father had it at almost the same age." She asked, "Could I get hold of the hospital records?" A great question. What she was really asking me is, why am I keeping myself in this historical rut? So I say, without even thinking about it, "I can do better. I can get hold of his physician." What the hell, he had been my physician, too, when I was a teenager. His younger son is a Park Avenue attorney, and when the secretary told him a rabbi was on the phone regarding his father, he thought immediately that someone was calling to tell him his father had died. Is death always there just below the surface ready to spook us all?

If I get through all this, today is a day I shall never forget. I spoke to Joe, the doctor of my youth. Just hearing his voice—it was absolutely the same—was a comfort. In retrospect he was the voice of reason in my youth, and maybe also my model for research and knowledge. And he heard of my condition with such calm. Eighty-two years old and absolutely lucid. He has nothing to do but read medical journals and take care of all his friends. I told him how worried I was about the collateral circulation picking up because of all the occlusions, and he said, "Don't worry, once the circulation builds up, it can blow open some of the collateral."

Why didn't someone else tell me of that possibility? But the most incredible thing is what he told me about my father—God bless Florence, my father did not have angina. His problem was the heart muscle itself. Joe said that my father's cardiograms never showed arterial problems, and even his death was not "caused" by the heart but a bizarre kind of pneumonia that infected his already weakened heart. He died of endocarditis. All the time I was simply remembering his difficulty in walking, losing his breath easily, one of his doctors saying that he had a body of a man ten years older that had lost the reserve power of his heart. But my tests show that if anything I have a body of a man ten years younger, that the strength of my heart muscle is very good, and I am much better prepared to deal with tension and anxiety. Somewhere there may a similarity, but in their key difference lies a path for individual responsibility. A genetic ghost has been exorcised.

Five days to go until the operation.

What further irony. Today two physician friends of mine brought over Halberstram's interview of Debakke on coronary bypass just published in *Modern Medicine.* Debakke says two things which, with the knowledge I now have, is terribly reassuring about my chances on this thing. One, that the operation is contraindicated when the occlusions are low in the artery bed. (Thank God I stole a copy of the map.) The big ones for me are at the top of my arteries. Second, that it's not an advisable operation if the index of ejection (what I have been calling the power of the heart) is below about 20 percent. But mine is a whopping big 88 percent. That is precisely where my heart "condition" differs from my father's. I'm fully equipped, and I'm ready.

Tomorrow's the day and I feel strangely calm. I guess it's because I feel I have done everything I could. I got my relationship system going and prepared my family emotionally and financially, I obtained all the knowledge I could to make myself feel confident, and I'm already thinking of this as a detour, a vacation, something after which I can get back on the road to my goals. Even my plans for how to deal with the medical institution seem to have worked: the clinical interest and the humor. And right up to the end. A member of the anesthesiology team came in this evening to ask questions. By now I had told the story so often I had reached the point of inadvertently using medical terminology all over the place, correctly for that matter. She thought I was a doctor! Then I said to her, "Do you want to see the map?" "Oh, yes," she says gleefully. I had forgotten about all the statistics listed on the attached page, and she says, "Unbelievable, wait till they see what I have!" Good God, don't these specialists talk to one another? But the real funny part was the guy who came in to shave me. He obviously had a date and figured it would take about ten minutes. Furry me, it took forty minutes, and I kept joking like crazy for fear he'd slip.

AFTER THE OPERATION

I have just gone through the two worst days of my life. But who cares? I'm alive!

They took the last tubes out today and I got out of bed, even walked a little. They're encouraging me to walk. I'm afraid I'll pull the grafts out and my body cavity will fill up with blood. On the other hand I've never heard of that happening to anyone else. And some of the other guys (why is it only guys?) are walking along the halls like they were just in here for tests. Hearing about or noticing the others is really a two-edged sword: on the one hand, you see their successes and hear about their experiences and it gives you hope, prepares you some for the worst, but every now and then you hear about someone who didn't make it. How did that line go from that old Dr. Kildare movie? "The operation was a success, but the patient died." There's more to healing than healing.

I made it to the end of the hall today and tomorrow I'll try to the next wing. Got a kick out of walking my visitors to the door! Not the door of the room but those swinging ones down the end of the hall. It's really incredible how strength returns. (Where does it go when it's away?) Funny thing is, I'm really not in much pain. There's

almost no pain at all around the incision, and that in itself is so incredibly small. How did they all get their hands in there? Good
God, they must have taken the thing out. And I got to see the incision the day after, no bandages like what it used to be like when I
was a kid. I expected to wake up dressed like a mummy and here I
was so worried about my allergy to adhesive tape. The incision in
the leg where they took out the veins is five times longer than the
wound in the chest. No wonder I hear about people having more
trouble with their leg. But the only real pain is when I cough. They
say I'll feel that resonating of my heart sack for months, especially
on rainy days. I've turned into an aneroid barometer! Now if I can
only figure a way of maintaining such sensitivity to the world about
me.

I made it down to the other ward today—in fact, I got two wards
farther. May have overdone it a little, but at least by counting wards
I am setting up a way of measuring and monitoring progress. But
I'm not making any progress on that breathing machine: I just can't
get the thing to go up no matter how hard I blow, and it makes me
cough. I better do it, though—I don't want any complications. I'll
bet some people are going better on this thing and can't walk at all.
Hell, maybe if you walk, you don't need to try this.

The incident over the smoking today really focused an important
issue for me. People were violating the No Smoking signs in the hall
and me with an allergy to smoking generally, trying not to have to
sneeze. Yet as angry as I was about this irresponsibility and the attitude of some of the nurses who say they can't do much about it, I
managed to control myself. I did not go into a rage; I did not attack
anyone; I did not harbor ill feelings. I did make one call to the supervisor but declined her invitation to follow it up further (thus
staying out of the middle of whatever shtick she had). This is what
I have got to keep doing. It is becoming clear to me that this confrontation with my mortality is going to enable me to do things I
have never been able to do, or at least stick to.

Tomorrow I go home. It's incredible. I'm healing so fast. And I'm alive. That's the important thing. Still can't get over all the well-wishers, the cards, the presents. I just never thought that many people cared. And my cousin (my best man at my wedding) is flying down from Canada to see me home. Would I have done that for him? One can walk down the halls counting the cards on the wall and get a picture of the patient's relative degree of isolation, though in truth that's only one kind of isolation. The ones with the most cards are probably people-pleasers and they're often more isolated than true loners. Ten to twenty-five cards is the good range, way over or under and you've got problems. But I'm going home, six days later. I made it, that's the important thing, and I've got a "new heart."

I walked a mile today. I've measured out several half-mile radii from my house, and I'll go to different ones each day. It takes me about thirty-five minutes and it's painful, but what exhilaration! I can feel my whole body loosening up. I never realized walking affects so many muscles. And it clears the head—I had forgotten that one.

Did it in less than thirty-five minutes today. Still having trouble with my memory: I get an idea and then later all I remember is that I'd gotten one. It'll get better though. That's the difference, death simply wipes out all the facts, obliterates the stored ideas, makes our concepts unrecognizable. Zip—and its all blank. One works for years to store them, manipulate them, rearrange them, is perhaps on the very edge of wholly original new frameworks for them, and then zap, and it's all blank. Death is pushing the erase button.

It rained today so I walked in the house. The floors of the shopping malls are too hard. Forty-eight times around the middle floor is a mile. When I walk indoors it's like doing laps, and each time I come by the digital clock I get a reading on my progress. If only we had something cyclical like that in life—yearly readings for measuring our progress. But then, what's progress? For me it's easy: how many laps I can do in a minute, an hour? How far I can walk in a half-hour? How long it takes me to catch my breath.

I'm still fascinated by this feedback loop. It's got to be there in all of us and we just don't pay attention to it. Actually I started it before the operation, in those last few weeks when I know I was close, when the pains would come just from walking a slight incline and I couldn't even carry books to the car without starting to feel something. Even though the doctor said, "All we are trying to do is prevent damage to the heart muscle before the operation," and I had nitroglycerine on me, I never took a pill. My reasoning was that I wanted maximum awareness of the state of my arteries. I decided that if the pains came on I would freeze, not make a move, and if they lasted more than fifteen minutes I would take one. But they never did. Of course I did a lot of getting motionless, but boy, was I tuned in. And again that may be the key to the Type A personality. Not that we are so aggressive, but that perhaps because of that aggressiveness, we are not tuned in.

More on aggressiveness. The way I am attacking my condition is aggressive. What's wrong with that? It's that old confusion in our society again, particularly among those who hide their aggressiveness and want to take down those who are. We confuse initiative and hostility. How well I remember that course at the Washington School of Psychiatry in which everyone kept using the word *aggressive* to mean *hostile.* I didn't know about social workers in those days, and I would get up and say, "Aggressive is not the adjectival from of aggression. Aggressionistic is. Similarly, aggression is not the noun form of aggressive, aggressiveness is." And when they came out of their stupor, they all said I was playing with words. In a sense I was, but their heads weren't clear. It's a terribly important distinction both for limiting drive and for allowing it to continue, with oneself and with others (in particular, one's kids). Hey, speaking of clear heads, mine is getting clearer every day.

I am getting so much out of this walking. Every day is a bonus. Nothing like facing one's own mortality for coming to appreciate life. But I wonder how long it will last. Twice in my life I had anaphylactic reactions to penicillin. After each I sat under the trees and watched the sun go down and vowed to appreciate life. Those vows lasted exactly forty-eight hours. But I think this one is different—in part because of where I am now in my life's course, in part because of the severity and the length of time of the threat. Also, let's face it, the threat has really not gone away.

More on vows. In the past, whenever I was facing a crisis I often made a kind of vow. Something like, "If things turn out right, I will devote my life to—" or, "I will never again do this or that"—or, "I'll always. . . . " Like Jacob after seeing the angels on the ladder—"You do this for me and I will spread your message." But *this* time I did not do it, I made no vows. I thought about it, but I don't owe anybody anything (except my own). That's going to make a difference, I think. Funny part is, I always thought I was making that vow with the Eternal, and yet these bargains were kind of Faustian. Could it really be? I mean, I went down to hell and came back without a bargain. I'm free.

The last few days have been terrible. With the exception of a few hours spent with visitors, I am having so much trouble with my leg and my coughing. And I thought I was doing so well! I must have picked up some kind of infection. I have a little fever. My God, and I was doing so well. Am I going to relapse? I'm supposed to exercise for half an hour twice daily but I can't walk on the damn leg. It's swollen, there's some gout. Actually it's the foot. Does that mean the circulation isn't right? Maybe something's wrong after all with the arteries. And I thought I was doing so well. Don't even want to make notes in this diary anymore. What the hell has happened? I'm always telling my clients that progress is zigzag. I guess that's true here, too—I always seem to remember that in the past the first few days after surgery were bad but that it was steadily uphill after that, and then one day you wake up and it's like you never had any surgery at all. But I seem to have lost all my gains.

Went to the surgeons today. They say it's all natural. At least I got a lift from the discussion of my procedure. They said it all went off without a hitch. It never even occurred to me that there could be hitches—I mean, if you come out okay I guess that's what you call good team work, not the surgical team but my team, arteries in the middle, lungs on the end, and the heart at QB. We did it, fellas! But I alternate between constant dozing, lose hours at a time—and worrying about the foot. I can't concentrate on anything.

Only once before do I remember going through such pain, when I twisted an ankle and badly tore the ligaments and had to keep the leg horizontal to prevent the blood from flowing down. There I was—lying in my bed, a senior in college ready to go to Washington on a transfer program, stuck in a back bedroom, and all the while my father dying in the next room with my mother completely caught up with him. The only time I seriously considered suicide. But I got through it, I got down to Washington, and my father died nine months later.

I can't get over the extent to which this whole process has been a rite of passage, which are not to be equated with the ceremonies themselves but with the period of six months to a year around them. How they function as "hinges of time," and affect the relationships of all who go through them. It's not just being cute to say that an operation is the ceremony. Because there is a person to be celebrated, there's a high priest and his entourage who all wear robes. It takes a couple of hours: the preparation, the main part, and the "closing." There are traditions which must be abided by—those that belong to the whole denomination, to that particular rite, and to that particular church. Sometimes there are pews for onlookers, and there's often music in the background. There is even the presence of the supernatural: the heart-lung machine.

Being alive is somewhat eerie. I realize that what I went through has almost become routine, but there is still an almost ethereal quality to it that I keep associating with the heart-lung machine. I'll bet it's the aspect of the operation most people want to know about. I remember wanting to see it when I came into the operating theater—it's the real star of the show. In effect they put you to death for about half an hour. The heart never completely stops, they just stimulate it to the point that it's barely thumping. But during that half-hour they have bypassed your two most vital organs. There's the real bypass. During that time you are not running you and when they connect you up again, it's literally a rejuvenation. You are coming back to life. Hell, you're being reborn. "Tell me, Frankenstein, how did it feel when that charge brought you to life?" "Well, it took a while for me to get used to my new body." Yes, I know, but wasn't it kind of eerie?" "Absolutely, that's why I'm so good at playing these weird parts."

More on the matter of pain. I understand that during the operation they ask the relatives in the waiting room what to tell the patient when he wakes up so that the shock and anxiety will be minimal. In my case, my wife said, "Explain to him everything you're doing." So when it was all over and she came into intensive care to see me, she said, "I passed an arc of several other patient cells and saw the same scene each time: the patient still dead to the world, the relatives outside talking in hushed tones, the medical staff silently scurrying about." Then she comes to mine, and I'm sitting there eyes wide open, and everyone talking a mile a minute. I was more aware than those other poor bastards, but they sure missed a hell of a lot of pain. Now what more could you want for a metaphor of life?

The thought for today is inflammation. It is amazing how the body's defense system can be more destructive than the disease it's a response to. On the one hand, you have to do something about it or it will incapacitate you, if not do you in altogether; on the other hand, you can't let it run you. I've been thinking that how in my work with families, what I'm dealing with for the most part is inflammation, whereas the clients all think what is bothering them is the wound. In other words, if the analogy holds true then medicine is the art of enabling the body to do what comes naturally—to heal. My clients come in focused on the wound instead of on their anxiety and reactivity, which is the inflammation. Perhaps just telling them this would enable them to refocus. For it certainly has been my experience that if parents can reduce their reactivity and anxiety to a child's problem, the "wound" tends to heal itself. Though there is one way in which the analogy does not hold, or at least I do not know enough about medicine or anatomy or physiology to know if it holds. When a family or a family member does get hold of its own inflammation, the child with the wound at first appears to get worse and it is necessary for the rest of the family to try even harder to control their inflammatory responses. I don't know if something like that happens in physical medicine, but maybe it's just a matter of how you define the wound.

A rather remarkable thing occurred last night. I woke up and decided to check out something my post-op booklet said, and as I was leafing through the pages looking for the paragraph, I burst into tears. It was the little cartoon character of the heart patient walking hand-in-hand with his heart. But I didn't just tear up, or burst into tears and stop. I cried repeatedly for ten or fifteen minutes. There was some self-pity, and feeling of camaraderie with my little friend whom I almost lost (hell, it almost lost me). But it was also, of course, something much bigger than I will ever be able to fathom—the release of something far more complex than tension. I associate it with the witch in *Bell, Book, and Candle,* who can't cry and can't love either. And then there's this dramatic moment when because of her feelings, she doesn't even realize she has tears come down her cheek. Talk about major surgery. Something very major has happened to me.

RECUPERATION

This has clearly been the watershed of my life. The streams and currents of all my thought processes, all my paths, all my goals and wishes have merged into one pool dammed up by this crisis, and now it's up to me to decided how to let the flow come out again. I mean in which directions, to what extent, and with what force. Like all crises, it is an opportunity. It's clear to me that I must make my first goal my own health—and happiness. That addendum there after the dash is a new one for me. I have never really thought about my happiness, just my functioning. Second come my kids. What if they had lost me? It would not have been the end of the world, and they might have even wound up with a better father. But I have so much to offer them, so much knowledge and wisdom and experience and love. So much of the time I have felt, "What has all my learning been for if not to pass on?" and it almost got bypassed. Third would be my own career. I think that is a new one also, to put it after my kids. But what does it mean to switch priorities? How does it work out in practice? Is it a matter of time invested, time spent, emotion invested, emotion spent? Where one puts or directs one's thoughts? Maybe it shows up at moments of decision. But the first decisions must be the order of priorities.

My God, I am feeling better than I have in ten years. People are saying I look ten years younger, too! This must have been coming on for an awfully long time and affecting other bodily processes as well. It could be just the loss of weight or the additional exercise that is making me feel and look better, or my attitude. After all, I just won a victory over something. Also, I haven't had a vacation that long in twenty years—and it was a vacation, too, in spite of the anxiety and pain. In the denotative sense of the word, everything got *evacuated*. Of course, one of the dangers of evacuating is the vacuum it creates, which always sets up the possibility of getting sucked into something too fast. There is no need to fill it up immediately.

Today I went to a bookstore and looked through eight different diet books, all written by physicians, all claiming to know what is really best for you, and each having a different approach. That part is okay—what is not okay is that each proves its view with a scientific study. How the hell is a layperson supposed to make objective decisions if doctors are more concerned with their approach than with the truth? It's no different from religion or politics or psychotherapy. But I guess there are many patients who just want to be told what to do, and the funny thing is that the truth may not matter. Maybe all that matters is that you believe in something or someone. I have never been a faddist and the Pritikin system, as helpful as it might be for some people, just turns me off. It's too much like a cult. Which I must admit maybe just right for certain kinds of emotionally dependent people (aren't we all?).

Yet there must be something to this. Just the other day a middle-aged woman told me how some therapist (among the finest I have ever known) busted up her marriage. Then later she tells me that her father has been a sworn advocate of the Pritikin diet for several years since his bypass. Somehow there is a relationship between those two, the lifesaving and blaming attributed to authority.

Today I made a list of everything I'm intense about and to see them all at once was really revelatory. I get uptight, furious, desirous of defending my territory, rights, or soul far more quickly—no, automatically—than I had any idea. It's really pervasive, like the arterial blockage. That damn blockage all over my system is a metaphor of the extent to which I let my entire life be blocked by experiences where I am challenged. Of course, I'm not really challenged. I only (hah, only!) perceive it that way. It's a kind of paranoia. But I am doing better. Actually it's amazing—here I am a therapist and know that it takes time to change behavior patterns. Yet somehow I thought that just making the vow not to get so intense would be the way to do it. That's only the benchmark. I will have to undergo many trials in which I will get too intense, but the key will be to recognize those moments and not let them carry me away.

Had my postoperative stress test today. (Like I haven't been having one every day.) Perfect, they said. Nine minutes with no sign of anything. "Must have connected you up right," the cardiologist opined. (I think he's still angry I didn't go to his alma mater for the surgery.) Actually, I trained for the test. Been walking up hills fast, wanted to break the damn machine, hear it cry "uncle." Wanted to be able to say, when he told me that was enough, "Can't you make it go faster?"

I am feeling so good that it has become harder to keep up with my resolve. Every now and then I get some twinge somewhere, and all the anxiety conditioned by the previous experience flits by. On the other hand, these twinges are healthy reminders. It is clearer than ever how difficult it is going to be to stick with my changed habits of eating and exercise, no less to work on the stress when I have lost all pain completely.

Today I saw my son score his first goal. It was so exciting—a penalty shot, but what the hell, a goal! He hasn't shown great athletic prowess and the goalie was so prepared, but he just moved up on him slowly and then zip, before the goalie knew what happened, it was under his stick. What a terrific thing to live for—the goal, his face, the encouragement and congratulation of his teammates. And me cheering him on.

Went back to see the surgeon today. I was looking forward to it, wanted to tell him how grateful I was and maybe shoot the breeze a little—after all, I've known one of his staff for a long time. But he didn't know who I was. My mistake was I thought he'd recognize my face. If I could have entered inside out, there would have been no problem; it would have been "Hi there, quadruple-with the intra cardiol-cross-canal connection without complications!" Well, some people just have no memory for faces.

If western civilization had conceived of the seat of the emotions to be in the liver rather than the heart, would we all be having liver at-tacks? Of course, if too much cholesterol is really a dysfunction in the liver, then maybe a heart attack is really a liver attack. Look at all the similes and metaphors in the English language which place our emotions in the heart.

It is truly amazing to what extent an entire family functions as an organism. From the moment I got my diagnosis, the health of my wife and kids has been absolutely great. Here and there the kids in particular seem to suffer some little ailment (due to anxiety, no doubt) but nothing lasts more than a day. And now the opposite—on the day we came back from the Bahamas, when I was returning to my old energy and able to walk indefinitely, my wife, who had been in great shape throughout this crisis, started to cough and has been fatigued for six weeks. It could be the let-down phenomenon, where individuals seem to hold off colds and other things until the crisis is over. Actually I once saw a lecture showing that individual different endocrine levels peaked or reached their nadir during tense periods but that the peak or the nadir occurred just after the crisis was over. From an organic systems point, however, the suggestion is just too strong that an illness in a family keeps the others healthy, and not just because they are rising to the occasion.

I remember reading that Joe Kuharich, former coach of the Eagles and the Redskins, said after he got his diagnosis of cancer how much he had to fight off his family's efforts to be overhelpful. He got a positive reaction rather than a negative one, but somehow it was the same. The really scary thing is this: if we assume that in some way almost every life-threatening illness is somaticizing the emotional intensity or chronic anxiety in the family, then full return to strength and health can be more disruptive to the family than death! Perhaps it's easier to bury someone than to divorce them.

As I look back on the past couple of years, maybe longer, I think that I lost my nerve. I used to have dreams and goals and be unafraid to pursue things with risk. While I remained too quick to accept minor challenges, I did not go after big ones. And maybe it was my mother's death: I functioned in some way for her, and when she died I lost my motivation. But I must get my mad-dog persistence back, although not in some out-of-control way. The gambling I did in the Bahamas really shook up the family. It wasn't much, considering the total cost of the trip, but it disturbed them so at first. Then they came to love it. The fact of the matter is, however, that what distinguished Columbus from the other was not his insight or his courage, but his mad-dog persistence. I must not "go gently into that good night."

More on control. The research of my colleagues on the emotional aspects of cancer keeps coming up with material around the issue of control. I felt I had lost control, as many cancer patients report feeling in the year before the onset of the disease, and yet giving up control can also be a way of taking control. One cancer patient reports that immediately after the diagnosis, she says, "I have got to take control of my life," and she does well; another says, "The hell with everything, I quit," and he also does well. There is a difference between loss of control and giving up control. The other side of controlling is not loss of control, but chaos. I mentioned this to a client of mine who suffers from severe asthma attacks. When I asked her if she could give up control without becoming chaotic, she responded, "That's the story of my life!" And yet when I look at that map of my arteries, even though it seems to signify a loss of control, still, letting go is somehow the ultimate form of taking charge.

Today was an important day—I did my first major workshop since the operation. In fact it was the very one I had to cancel in order to take the stress test back in October. Today thus marks the end of the passage. It was the final rite. I had a great audience, perhaps because in some way these people went through the passage with me because of the cancellation.

But there was something, something different about the way I presented—something to do with humility and patience. I took more time to let things develop and talked more personally. I felt more of a sense of wonder, a confession of what I didn't know, the thrill of the search.

I remember once when a large tree was cut down by a neighbor. They planted a young sapling near it to take its place and I thought to myself, "It sure will take a long time—a century, really, to replace it." But after a year its root system had hooked up with what the big tree had left behind and it grew phenomenally. It will still take a century, but its first ten to twenty years are going to be unbelievable. That's the way I felt about myself after today. I have a new root system, but it can hook up with and get the benefit of the old, and I shall combine the best of both. Indeed, I shall not go gently into that good night.

How to Get Your Parent into a Nursing Home Without Turning Gray in the Process

This essay and the following show Friedman's preoccupation with putting his theories into practice with regard to his family relationships, including his own self-management in the face of others' illness and anxiety and his effort to work with the triangles that exist in any family system.

My mother had been fainting periodically. A year ago she broke her hip and then, at seventy-six, she had just undergone a series of operations designed to clean her arteries from the plaque and accompanying embolisms which the doctors thought might be causing the episodes. She had become terribly confused and disoriented in the hospital, and the doctors suspected that the confusion might be the result of actual brain deterioration, not just the dislocation of an unfamiliar setting which, along with the anesthesia, can often seem to make the aged go out of their heads. My mother should have constant medical supervision, they felt, at least during the first month or two she was out of the hospital. So it was decided that she should convalesce in a nursing house rather than try to live alone—as she

145

had been doing for the past two decades in her mid-Manhattan apartment.

The hospital, of course, was prepared to help through its social service programs, but when I found that the social workers made recommendations largely on the basis of brochures and hearsay, and generally had not themselves actually visited the homes, I decided that I didn't need a "travel agent" who made recommendations on the basis of travelogues. I rented a car, therefore, and early one weekend morning drove up into Westchester to find a suitable nursing home for my mother. I had decided on Westchester because my mother had old friends and relatives in that direction, and I had already begun a process of frequent calls to these individuals to involve them more and to create a corps of visitors.

As I weaved my way up the beautiful Bronx River Parkway that morning, I had one major criterion in mind that would help me decide, aside from the usual concerns of competence and cleanliness. I have always believed that all physiological processes are affected, to some extent, by the emotional atmosphere in which they take place. Opportunities for recuperation are optimized (like opportunities for growth, I believe) when those in the caring position—parent, child, doctor, or nurse—are on the side of challenge rather than comfort. I had always tried to teach parents who came to see me for help with their children that their children would start to function better if the parents could get their own thresholds for their children's pain to increase. In a lecture at a medical school I even suggested that, given a group of doctors who were the same in every respect, those with the fastest convalescent rates would actually be those with the highest threshold for their patients' pain. Assuming that I could do nothing about whatever undeterminable physiological processes were going on in my mother, and finding that the doctors could in no way be sure to what extent her symptoms were the result of physiological rather than emotional processes, I decided I had nothing to lose by erring myself on the side of challenge.

My first destination was a home that had been recommended to me by some professional people I knew in the Westchester area. They said it had a terrific rating for good medical care, though they warned me (foreshadowing the entire day) that the owner was a pretty sharp businessman. He was, in fact, I was told later, about to be indicted for forcing families to go through unneeded family therapy sessions which increased the Medicare payments.

I had called in advance and the intake social worker seemed quite efficient. I also had heard that the place was away from the city, which I took to mean a rural setting; since I knew my mother hated institutions, this sounded good. To my surprise, I found it situated instead on the corner of a residential neighborhood which, perhaps because of the contrasts with surrounding buildings, emphasized its institutional appearance. Ms. Powell (a pseudonym) saw my disappointment immediately and reassured me that they had a garden where my mother could sit when it got warm. This was mid-December and I had clearly told her on the phone I was only looking for a two- or at best three-month convalescent stay.

After Ms. Powell ushered me into her office and I began to explain what I was looking for, she started taking notes, which she placed immediately into an official record as though I were already committed to her establishment. At times she even broke in to correct my view of what my mother was going through, so that I finally had to say to her, "Look, I am trying to give you an idea of my philosophy of recuperation so I can know something of yours, and you keep trying to argue me out of my perceptions." At this she let up somewhat and began to show me around the various wings, stressing the fact that each section dealt with individuals who were capable of a different degree of functioning. All during this interview she kept saying things like, "Mom will find this comfortable" and "Mom would probably like this." Perhaps because I am an only child, the sibling-like relationship the social worker seemed to be trying to establish with me was at the very least unfamiliar. The only other time I had ever heard this way of talking about someone else's mother was from an undertaker. After a while she must have read my mind and began saying "your mother," but habits are hard to break, I guess, and she lapsed back into calling her "Mom."

I asked if the nursing home (I actually slipped and referred to it as a hospital) was concerned with moving people up the ladder of functioning and was assured, "Definitely." Again, trying to emphasize the recuperation aspect, I mentioned that I had noticed only elderly people, and if this was in fact a convalescent home as well as a nursing home for the aged, how come everyone was so old? I was assured that people did leave the home for other reasons than death, but when I asked what percent, was given no answer; when I pressed the point from another direction by asking the average age of the clientele, I was told the inmates ranged from sixty to ninety years old. "The average age?" I asked again. "Eighty-two" was the answer, finally. Finally, as I was leaving, Ms. Powell asked me if it would be all right to contact the family doctor to get all the information that would be needed. I was forced to leave with a "Don't call me, I'll call you" kind of response and hit the road for the only other place in the area I knew by reputation.

The second place I visited seemed ideologically on the other end of the continuum. Set on a huge rural estate, it had connections with a hospital system and was dedicated solely to rehabilitation. One could not stay there more than four months and in fact would get kicked out once the staff perceived the patient not to need them anymore. Everything about the place seemed right; the family doctor was quite sure they would accept my mother initially but—and here was the rub—acceptance in no way guaranteed continued residence. What if, after a week, it was determined that my mother didn't need or couldn't use them? Clearly I could not rest assured with any satisfaction with this institution when things were going to be on a month-to-month or week-to-week observatory basis about my mother's ability to function independently.

By now it was already past lunchtime and I was running out of time. At this point I remembered Ma Bell, whipped out the Yellow Pages, and started feverishly copying down addresses of nursing homes, mapped out directions to several with the help of a local policeman, and bolted westward. Arriving at a new high-rise, I was ushered around by a man older than my mother who showed me that they did indeed have different floors for different levels of functioning. I was impressed that the place would use their own inhabitants to help explain the way they worked; the atmosphere was generally gay and resembled the kind of place my grandmother used to go for the summers. Also, the fact that it was new meant, I understood, it was more likely that they would have vacancies. On my yellow pad, which was now developing into a cross-reference table, therefore, I placed a check.

(The check became a cross, however, the following Monday when I called the business office and was told they could only hold a bed for two days. I pointed out that such a length of time was quite unreasonable, given all the planning involved in moving her out of the hospital, but they said, "We have a waiting list and just can't do any better." A pause followed. "Unless—you are willing to pay for the room from the time you reserve it." What about the waiting list, I thought, and said, "That certainly sounds like money under the table to me." The response? "We would only do this as a favor to you.")

So, thinking I had found a place with possibilities, I now headed east again, past the two homes I had already seen, clear over to the other end of the county where, for the first time, I met an administrator who thought exactly the way I did. She agreed totally with my desire not to let my mother become too dependent; she sympathized with what I had found elsewhere and she explained that here they had two distinct facilities. One was for those who need constant medical supervision and one was, as the technical term went—"health related." In the latter, housed in a separate building, people stayed who could take care of all their needs except perhaps cooking. I pointed out that my mother was somewhere in the middle and asked if she started out in the medical facility, would she be graduated to the other if she showed the ability to function independently? The reply which I received was like the answer to a dream: "We consider it a failure," she said, "if we are unable to move people to the health-related facility." Unfortunately, they did not expect to have a vacancy for months.

It was now 2:30 and, with two hours of light left, I still did not feel I had accomplished anything. But the administrator here was extremely helpful. She said that because of their no-vacancy situation, she was doing a lot of referring and produced a paper made up by a New York State health authority that listed all the approved homes in the county, pointed out to me that, with her experience, she would have started putting her mother on a waiting list the day she went into a hospital, and advised me to go to places that were the newest—of which she recommended three. At the same time she cautioned me that this was all on the basis of what others had told her. I called several places from her office to see if anyone was present at the other homes, thanked her profusely for her sincerity (of course, there's nothing like a full house to remove the competitive edge), promised her feedback on what I found, and zoomed up the New England Throughway, zipped around the Cross-Westchester, and headed toward the Tappan Zee Bridge.

Shortly after 3:00 I arrived at an estate quite isolated in the woods that had once belonged to one of Hollywood's famous. A brand-new, motel-like facility had just been constructed, and older buildings which had formerly housed the patients were being gutted and reconstructed for a health-related facility. The beauty of the place was unsurpassed, and the administrator was both helpful and understanding. It appeared that they had room and I was much impressed by the facilities and the programs. We walked in on twenty elderly patients in a painting class. From the point of view of care the place got an A on my chart, and I began to realize that the beauty of a place might also encourage more visits from friends and relatives. On the other hand, the health-related facility was about a year from completion, and in terms of my mother's recuperation schedule, that was equivalent to a light year. At present, it was quite obvious that almost nobody left this place except in a coffin.

The administrator had given me directions back to New York and at 4:00 p.m. it certainly seemed too late to try anymore. I was tired. I had at least found a place that was acceptable and how different could any other place be, anyway? On the other hand, this was my last chance. Even if I found no one left at one more I really wanted to see, I could always talk to them on the phone once I had actually seen the place. So I ignored the directions back to New York and headed north through towns that were more familiar twenty-five years ago, on a journey of recollections from my childhood of summer camps and Rip Van Winkle.

I should also mention that the entire trip became a cram course in medical economics. Final exam question: discuss the differences between Medicare and Medicaid, showing that you understand the economic, sociological, and philosophical ramifications of each as well as how each operates and how each in turn can be defrauded. Medicare, I learned at one place, paid for nursing home stays only if there was rehabilitation involved or constant medical supervision could be justified. It was not for custodial care, I learned elsewhere. Still, it only paid for the first twenty days in full, after which private plans would have to take up the slack. It was, however, someone pointed out, fully democratic and required no vows of poverty.

Medicaid, on the other hand, I came to learn, was a horse of a different color. It paid for everything, for life, provided you were lucky enough not to have any money of your own. At that point some interesting ironies began to show. My mother, always an industrious individual, had worked until she was seventy-two, even lying about her age so she could keep her job. She never wanted to be dependent, and wanted to make sure there would always be money for an emergency. Now she was dysfunctional for the first time in her life, and her previous functioning was going to contribute to a larger pot for people who had been relatively dysfunctional for most of their healthy lives.

At 4:30, in the gloaming, I arrived on a hill overlooking the Hudson and thought that the place was so beautiful even I would not mind dying there. It was so late when I arrived that the administrator passed me going out as I entered, and she had just left. Again, it was the same story: they were set up for the dysfunctional and the semi-dysfunctional. The place was well-run and they had no need to keep someone dependent—but as I had now learned, when you find them, they have no room. The administrator again was extremely helpful. "Call me when you are ready to move your mother—maybe we can do something." (Another invitation for under-the-table money? Or was my increasing anxiety over getting something settled making me paranoid?) Actually this place was pure class—it had not even opted for Medicare, since they did not want a lot of turnover—but somehow I felt the concern for class was overriding, and the same lack of need to find people would keep them from needing to retain people. We left on the best of terms and she even told me one more stop not far away, on my way home, which I made as the last streak of sun pulled the shade of darkness down over the Palisades. Once again they were graded for different levels of functioning, and once again, when I later called from home to speak to the business office, I found they had a waiting list.

Three days later I called the social worker who was an expert on nursing homes at my mother's hospital. She had been on vacation while I was in New York and the social worker assigned to my mother had given me her number, but wasn't sure whether the expert would speak to patient families directly. I told her what I had done and asked for her comments, corrections, or additions.

"You have the whole picture," she said. "There's nothing I can add. I wish every family would do this so they would know."

"Well," I said, "maybe I'll write it up so they will!"

The place I finally chose was part of a large state hospital system, which by law had to kick you out after a month. While there was no way of knowing how long my mother would need medical supervision, at least here society had by law forcibly protected its members from its "goodness." As it turned out, she did not even need the full month. For as soon as she got there her confusion was replaced by depression—a sign she was back to reality. Actually the very place I chose had created the right kind of challenge. My mother always had an avoidance reaction to cripples on the street. Thrust into the midst of what was basically an orthopedic convalescent center, she might as well have been in a frontline battlefield hospital, and all she could think was, "Get me out; I don't belong here!"

Old Age:
Condition or Diagnosis?

This essay describes how Friedman put his theories into practice while helping her mother in her older years.

In October 1974, my mother, age seventy-six, who had worked till seventy-two and lived alone quite independently since my father's death sixteen years previously, was hospitalized and diagnosed with advanced "cerebral-vascular arteriosclerosis, organic mental syndrome, and arteriosclerotic cardiovascular disease." She had been blacking out with increasing frequency and could not live alone any longer. It was also thought that two operations to catheterize both her major arteries to the brain might, on the one hand, retard the periodic episodes of oxygen insufficiency causing the fainting spells, and, on the other, remove the plaque which from time to time might be breaking off and, like small knives, destroying brain cells as they were carried upward. After the first operation, my mother's response to the anesthesia was to become terribly confused and disoriented. After the second operation, two weeks later, she seemed hopelessly psychotic.

This essay will describe my efforts over the next eighteen months to keep my mother functioning and to prevent her becoming another nursing home statistic. At first I was moved to make this effort because I believe that senility can be understood as a family process rather than simply one old person's disease or inevitable deterioration. Many of the efforts to be described, therefore, will show how I worked with other members of my mother's relationship system in an effort to modify the effects of her own natural aging. Once I became involved, however, unexpected events occurred in my own professional life which gave me an added reason to stay in the process. For I soon found that my deep involvement in my mother's extended family system brought me back into contact with forces that had done much to make me what I had become, and in turn were producing changes in myself that were quite unexpected. For example, early on I realized that I had to learn to deal successfully with the chronic anxiety that ping-ponged back and forth between my mother and her older sister, also a widow. They had played this game all their lives and had always lived within walking distance of one another. In fact, for the past fourteen years they had lived on the same floor of the same mid-Manhattan apartment house. Within weeks of my first successful effort at being able to stay in touch with that anxious system without becoming anxious myself, I suddenly found that almost every one of my client families had gone into crisis. For I had inadvertently become less anxious about their anxiety also.

Four theoretical assumptions helped me weather some of the more severe squalls encountered on this journey.

(1) Diagnosis
I have always held a deep distrust for diagnosis as an interpersonal transaction. Perhaps this stems originally from my intense study of religious thought and history so filled with appeals to authority as a way of avoiding verification. My own work with families and other forms of intense relationship systems, however, showed me over the years that far from being an isolated quirk of religionists, diagnosis as a means of destroying dialogue was a diffuse human phenomenon, particularly predictable, as anxiety in a system increases. In fact, it has always seemed to me that under such circumstances diagnosis, a tool which is a basic step in the quest for knowledge and scientific inquiry, becomes perverted to its opposite intent. What

in calmer times might have been a move to establish a hypothesis for further investigation now becomes a shield to ward off the sharp points of further questions, if not the sword-tip of modern inquisition as "sick" or "neurotic" replaces "heretical" or "unfaithful."

Thus alarm bells rang in the night when, after my mother was hospitalized, the following occurred. First, three specialists laid out my mother's future for me exactly, and stiffened in their attitudes toward me considerably whenever I tried to get them to explain more precisely what they meant by "chronic brain syndrome," no less how they could be so sure of the extent of her pathology. Second, my mother's former physician and close personal friend distanced himself from my mother even when I said, "Listen, she's got three older siblings, there are some constitutional reasons for hoping and trying." He responded to all my efforts with, "You have to remember she had a tougher life." Third, my mother's sister, in constant touch with the specialists and several other relatives, started talking "nursing home" and *about* my mother rather than *to* her.

I knew from the very beginning, therefore, that a major effort on my part would have to go in the direction of maintaining an independent perception of my mother and keeping people relating directly to my mother, even, as it turned out, when she herself tried to discourage our attempts. And all the way through she almost won me over to the other side.

(2) Rehabilitation

One of the perspectives that kept me on course was my view of the relationship between *psyche* and *soma*. I have never been comfortable with our society's conventional division between body and soul, and have tended to see the phrase *psychosomatic* as bringing together two parts that should never have been separated to begin with, a false dichotomy. I believe all physiological processes take place within an emotional climate that has varying effects on the course of any disease. This is obviously true when one talks about the patient's "attitude," but by extension it also has to mean the family's attitude as well. Indeed the onset of many diseases may require the satisfying of two conditions, one emotional and one physical. And individuals who might have satisfied one condition (emotional, viral, genetic) for years might not manifest a disease until the other condition was also satisfied.

The same views which have led me toward an organic view of any person's "human condition" have led me to an organic view of the family. Moreover, the fact that one is apparently dealing with a physical problem rather than an "emotional" one seems irrelevant. For it is impossible to know in advance to what extent the visible symptoms accompanying any physiological pathology are directly attributable to the extent of the pathology itself, or have been modified, for better or worse, by the overall emotional climate (by which I mean the family's emotional state, not just the patient's) in which that physiological process is occurring. It has always seemed to me, therefore, in situations of physical illness, one has nothing to lose by letting the doctors handle that side, and operating oneself in the area of the emotional, an area which could actually contain more variables.

No one functions at peak capacity throughout their lives. Actually most individuals probably do not function at much more than fifty percent of their capacity for most of their lives. When an individual has been diagnosed, however, there is a tendency to assume that the actual outer range of their functioning is the best they can do. All specific inabilities are then explained in terms of the patient's condition.

When this occurs, relatives, friends, and others helping the patient tend to move into the area of the patient's potential, thus preempting that space and treating the *actual* as the potential. Rehabilitation, convalescence, and therapy for the patient may begin, therefore, with the family—for example, reducing the anxiety or pity which moves family members to be so helpful. I have been struck, over the years, by one universal rule: if members of a family can increase their thresholds for another member's pain, that other member's threshold will also go up. Actually pain (and anxiety) is one of the best illustrations of the dangers of splitting off emotional from physiological processes when making a prognosis. For when pain increases or decreases, it is almost impossible to know whether it is due to a change in the stimulus or the threshold, which is influenced in turn, of course, by other factors such as isolation and dependency. Thus a major effort throughout the period to be described went into trying to reduce the overly helpful input of my mother's sister and others in her orbit.

(3) Support

Increasing the amount of available breathing space is only part of the problem, however. For it does not follow that just because the smothering is eliminated or reduced, that the patient will seek more air; often it is a waiting game, and the patient often can outlast the others. An additional effort on my part, therefore, was the attempt to stimulate my mother in her own behalf.

Two observations influenced my attitude here. The first is that the word "supportive" in our society tends to have the connotation "helpful," that is, to move in and allow oneself to be leaned on. I have seen little evidence to show that that kind of support will in itself contribute to a fundamental change in the needy one's ability to function better without it; usually the needy one's ability to change and the range of their functioning will always itself be limited by the helpful individual's ability to grow. I have therefore moved more and more both in my professional and family life toward a view of support which is framed in terms of challenge. But once again, the fundamental notions feed back into one another. For as I will show, my efforts to challenge my mother often increased the anxiety of other members of the family (and members of the helping professions as well), and in turn increased their efforts to "do" for my mother—which I came to see as doing her in.

The second observation has to do with the results I have seen in families with malfunctioning children when parents were able to get past the diagnosis of their child. In fact, I tell most such families that I have never seen a family achieve change in their child when they see their child as sick, which tends to evoke adaptive responses, but some have had success when they begin to think of the child as a spoiled brat who is taking them in. The parallel here has to do with an increasing phenomenon in our society: the child-become-parent to the parent who has now become their child. In most such situations, the children-now-become-parents assume a caretaking role. But if their own real children functioned the way their parents are now functioning, they would never let them get away with it. I thus decided that if my mother wanted me to be her father, I would treat her exactly the same way I treated my daughter. I would express my love and concern by erring on the side of pain, challenge, and growth.

(4) Anxiety

If there is one major factor in the emotional atmosphere of a rehabilitative process it is probably anxiety—that of the patient, the family, and those in the helping professions. In my own mind I have tended to use metaphors from electricity to understand how anxiety operates. For like electricity, its presence is almost only known by its effects, and like electricity its effects can seem both unpredictable and shocking unless one understands how the system operates. There are many other similarities also. Without stretching the metaphor too far, I mention one or two here because they indicate how I conceptualized much of what I was experiencing.

For example, it is possible to connect up electrical energy users so that each has an independent line to the electrical source (called parallel connections), or so that the source runs through each connection to get to the next (called a series connection). It has always seemed to me that some families are "connected up" more in series or more in parallel. In electrical circuits, when connections are made in parallel, if one element becomes faulty, it does not necessarily affect the others, whereas in a series, when one light goes out they all go out (families where trouble comes in bunches).

If members of a family connected more in series can develop more self, they do not get as "charged up" by what is happening to the others. Furthermore, in maintaining self at such moments, they actually seem to have circuit-breaking effects on the rest of the family.

A more specific example would be how I viewed the effects of my aunt's anxiety. I saw my mother's sister as an anxiety transformer— that is, anxiety currents would enter her at low levels of energy and, like a step-up transformer in an electrical circuit, always come out at levels twenty to fifty times higher.

But the two most important aspects of my analogizing anxiety to electricity are these. Just as it is impossible for an electric current to continue its potential without feedback, so anxiety in an emotional circuit requires feedback to maintain its energy level. This notion has led me to the conclusion that it is absolutely impossible for only one person in a family to remain anxious. But the other side of that is, if someone can become part of a highly anxious system of human connections without becoming anxious herself, the effect on the whole system is to act as a step-down transformer. As with transformers in an electrical circuit, one must be able to stay in touch with the system without becoming totally fused with it.

SOME FAMILY HISTORY

As I journeyed up to New York for the first of what would prove to be almost biweekly trips for the next half-year, I tried to review in my mind what had been happening in the family for the last few years. As we know today, what often appears to be the accidental or isolated eruption of a problem in one person can be the result of family transmission processes that have been in the works for months, years, or even generations.

In July of 1968 I had, through giving a surprise seventieth birthday party for my mother, spent several months trying to be a catalyst for changes in the family.[9] During that period I had reentered, so to speak, the family and established a position whereby, more than perhaps any other single member, I could relate and was in fact relating to almost every one of my mother's siblings and their children. Though as I learned from the family history I was putting together, it was most logical that I occupy that position. For I was born six months before my mother's father died, and his wife, my grandmother, soon moved in with us, where we shared the same room until I was a teenager. Even as a youngster I had occupied a special position among my mother's siblings, who always saw me

9. See "The Birthday Party" in Edwin Friedman, *The Myth of the Shiksa and Other Essays* (New York: Church Publishing, 2006), 123-46.

more than my cousins and always brought me a gift when they came
to visit their mother.

Over the ensuing years after the party, however, while I had
maintained some of my new contacts with aunts, uncles, and
cousins, several events transpired which had also caused cutoffs in
my relationships with others, particularly those closest to my
mother. One of the most important of these events involved my
mother's sister, her son, and their daughter. About a year after the
birthday party I became aware that my aunt was extremely anxious,
even for her. She began to imagine that she had cancer and was
dying.

I had once seen a family in which something like this occurred
precisely at the time that the older woman's only child, a son, got
closer to his wife. Suspecting something similar was happening, I
checked things out with my cousin and found that they were indeed experiencing some severely traumatic difficulties with their
daughter but that they were not telling his mother. When, months
later, I learned the true nature of the problem, I wrote my aunt a letter informing her of what they were keeping from her. Her condition cleared up almost overnight, but then a great gulf formed
between me and my cousin's family.

Shortly after this a second event occurred also regarding my
aunt. On a visit to the Washington area with my mother she saw a
copy of my article "The Birthday Party" and became so upset about
my revealing "family secrets" that from then on she would never let
me kiss her, and spiced all her conversation with sarcastic remarks.
Efforts to point out that members of the family could not be identified from the article, or that I had helped her by opposing the
keeping of significant secrets within the family, were of no avail. I
never did understand her reaction. While I had thought the giving
of the party was unthinkable in my family, writing it up appeared
to be totally unimaginable.

The third important family cutoff event of this period involved
a portion of my father's family who lived in Canada. Outside of my
mother's siblings, her sister-in-law and brother-in-law (my father's
brother) were her two most important relatives, perhaps even more
important than her own brothers. My uncle died about six months

after the party. The death occurred during an airlines strike and at
a time when I was not functioning very well myself. The complicated arrangements of getting to the funeral seemed too much of an
effort at the time, and I tried to show my concern through daily
phone calls instead. Evidently I had misjudged severely my own importance to that part of the family, misled, perhaps, by the fact that
they did not come to the party for my mother. For my cousin responded to all my comforting remarks icily. He would hear of no ex-
cuses, received all future calls coolly, and in effect cut off further
communication between our two immediate families, though I did
remain in periodic touch with his mother, my aunt. While I could
not prove in what way, if any, these family cutoffs might be contributing to the deterioration of my mother's health in recent years,
I did know from my work with families in general that the onset of
many pathological processes could be traced to cutoffs. I therefore
resolved that painful as it might be, and time-consuming as I
guessed it would be, I would have to make a significant effort toward the elimination of these ruptures in the family communication
system. Although I must also admit that I genuinely liked my relatives, wanted my growing children to have relationships with them,
and so, in many ways, saw the crisis as an opportunity.

Other major changes in the family during the previous several
years which I took into account were these. My mother's next older
brother (the only sibling who did not come to her party and who
had secretly married as a child) lost his wife and within a short period of time remarried a Catholic woman living in his apartment
building. My wife and I had a second child, a son. My mother retired at seventy-two from managing a wholesale showroom for children's clothes where she had worked most of her widowhood.

My own relationship with my mother had undergone somewhat
of a reversal. In previous years, indeed, most of my adult life, I had
been the one distancing myself from her efforts to be close, as well
as the partner in the relationship who was most easily made intense
and angry by many of the other's remarks. Now things in many
ways were the opposite. I genuinely wanted her friendship, only to
find her much less communicative. I found myself much looser in
the relationship generally, better able to tap the resources of wit and

playfulness largely inherited from her and her mother to keep me free of her anxiety while at the same time staying in the relationship. To my surprise, however, my success in changing my own functioning in the relationship did not always allow us to achieve the camaraderie I hoped for, as she often responded with anger or withdrawal.

In some ways this phenomenon originated in my parents' marriage. My father had been known as the hot-tempered one and my mother the soother, though even as a child I could see how she triggered him. When I stopped playing the same role in my relationship with my mother, her temper—almost totally unknown before— surfaced and I began to see for the first time how in many subtle ways my father's life, and death, were symptomatic of their relationship.

I realized therefore that it was also possible my mother's deterioration was in some ways a long-delayed reaction to the loss of the support of her husband—a delay caused by the fact that in large part, until recently, I had in unwitting ways filled the void.

THE PROCESS

What follows is a narrative of the most important events beginning in November 1974, when I first received word that my mother had been hospitalized, to April 1976.

(1) The Crisis
I first arrived at the hospital about 11:00 at night to find my aunt still visiting in my mother's room (the hospital is only two blocks from where they live and thus serves as an annex). I immediately encountered a pincers movement (a foreshadowing of the entire year) in which my mother acted childishly about her condition and the major decisions to be made while my aunt kept saying, "Just be nice to her." Within the next eight hours I had triggered fights with a security guard at the hospital, a cook in a diner, and an aide who was trying to clean my mother's room.

In an effort to loosen things up, I called the social worker assigned to my mother's case who, I was told, wanted to talk to me when I came to New York. She was of the "old school," however, or at least not of my school, and did little more than tell people what they had just told her. On the other hand, she was close to my age and I decided that if I involved her in the triangle between me, my mother, and her sister, she could be *my* sister.

The immediate problem confronting us was whether or not my mother should risk the operations the doctors had advised. They could not guarantee it would stop my mother's fainting spells, and they admitted a fair degree of risk. On the other hand, were the operations not performed there would be no way of knowing to what extent my mother's deteriorating state was due to the oxygen deficiency (a partially correctable problem) or organic brain deterioration, an apparently incurable situation.

I wanted my mother to make the decision. But to make it intelligently she would have to be informed of the true state of medical opinion about her condition, the risks, and the alternatives. What made it a problem was that she denied she was fainting, and her sister opposed upsetting her with the truth. I decided therefore to get the issue resolved through a family meeting in her hospital room between the three of us, but run by the social worker.

The worker arrived before my aunt, and I could see early that her interpretive style was going to be as effective as if her client were from another world. For example, at one point, before my aunt came in she was listening to my mother "shoot the breeze" about how her poor sister had to do so much for her. The worker immediately got therapeutic and said, "You mean your sister is a very nervous woman?" And my mother shot back, "Do you know a woman today who is not nervous?" Silence till my aunt arrived.

With the presence of a fourth party, my aunt seemed more reasonable and I was able to get more perspective. The conversation went all over the ballpark until I said to my mother, "This is the state of things and this is what has to be decided." But no one would take a stand. My aunt and the social worker were also telling my mother that she might have to give up her apartment, and kept warning her of the dangers of independence.

Finally my mother said, "I'll take my chances." This was what I was waiting for. I jumped in and said, "I support my mother in any decision she makes." During most of this session, however, the social worker got the pincers treatment as, each time she thought she had stabilized one of the ladies, the other seemed to switch on her. Outside in the hall later, I found her telling a doctor about the "incredible" session she had just had with my mother and aunt. I tried to reassure her, saying that it really had worked out very well and then added, "Hell, they're like any normal married couple." The next day a new social worker had been assigned to the case.

My mother came through both operations in excellent physical health. Unfortunately, the anesthesia and dislocation of a foreign setting (she had now been in the hospital a month) tipped the balance in what was already a precariously balanced cerebral system. At least that was the medical explanation given to me.

I was, however, beginning to pick up clues to other things going on that would turn out to be extremely helpful in the future. First, it was about this time that I noticed the stiffening of attitude toward me when I became too inquisitive about verification of diagnosis that equated my mother's emotional functioning with specific physiological states. One kindly specialist went so far as to say, "Let me tell you something. I have a mother with the exact same problem and I know. So I'm telling you not only as a doctor but as someone who's been there." In my own mind, however, I was saying to myself, "If you are going through the same problem, that makes you less of an expert, not more." I then found myself wondering if the former social worker, who was my age, was experiencing similar problems within her family—for the new one, who was younger, was operating with much more assurance, quite to the distaste of my aunt. This, however, would hardly be the last time I would get the impression that when certain professionals were dealing with my mother, they forgot whose mother they were dealing with.

Another clue which emerged at this time and which was to be a key to much of the future was the intensity of the relationship between my mother and aunt. I had always known they were close, but I had not realized that there was now almost no separation at all. Like two magnets close to one another which are kept apart because each is respectively attached elsewhere, my mother and aunt, after their husbands died, had slowly pulled and been pulled toward one another so that the resulting bond between the two was now infinitely more powerful.

My aunt, for her part, visited my mother every day and for most of the day, waiting on her hand and foot, and complaining that none of the other relatives visited and that the nurses didn't care, either. On the evening after each operation my mother in her confusion tried to get off the bed and go home, pulling down the intravenous tube with her. On each occasion this happened while talking to her sister. My aunt maintains that it was a good thing she was on the phone at the time and was able to call the hospital right back and warn them. But I was coming to the frightening realization that my mother was in some way programmed into certain stimuli from her sister.

Two other events during this crisis period turned out to have significant ramifications for later developments, one regarding my aunt and one my mother's general physician. I had realized the great importance of reworking my relationship with my aunt. While we were communicating in the effort to help my mother, she would not let that interfere with the official distance she was maintaining with me personally. On my second trip to New York, therefore, after I had heard her say she takes a drink of scotch every night to calm her nerves, I went out and bought the biggest bottle of the best scotch I could find. I came over to her apartment about nine at night with the huge bottle leaning against my shoulder looking like some Madison Avenue display. By ten we were talking about the weather, by eleven she was able to express her anger directly to me for the first time, and by midnight she was telling me secrets I had never heard about my own father.

The event regarding my mother's physician I cannot claim as much credit for, but its effect over the next year proved to be astounding. When I first met my mother's doctor and began asking him what caused the fainting, he explained how the "hardened" arteries would choke off the blood periodically and create an oxygen deficiency. I must have been in really good emotional shape at the moment (or else preoccupied), because it struck me that when fainting ensued, my mother was obviously in a position where the blood could then flow more easily and that was why the spells did not last long. In all events, I did not respond to the doctor's explanation in any anxious way, but said instead with ridiculously clinical cool, "Oh, that means the condition is self-corrective." The next day I got feedback from my mother, who seemed much better, about how impressed the doctor was with her son, and I realized an important principle: if members of a family can respond non-anxiously toward their relative's physician, the doctor in turn will function better with his patient.

It was during this period that I had begun to contact all my mother's friends and relatives, whether in New York, Canada, or California, and encourage them to contact my mother. But I also had to deal with the anxious perceptions of my mother, some of them coming directly from her sister, which in turn distanced my mother from her relatives and friends.

I had barely gotten to first base, however, in learning how to deal with my aunt's anxiety myself, even though I was sure learning what it did to those around her. On one occasion we went to the vault together to get my mother's bonds. (She had the other key to my mother's box, not I.) While there I thought it would be the responsible thing to use the occasion to look through all her papers. With each envelope I opened, my aunt said, "Be careful of this, put that back in the proper place, make sure you leave things as they are." Now priding myself on realizing what an anxious person she was, I tried not to react but concentrated on seeing just which papers of importance were there and decided I could come back alone and read them through. When I did come back alone, two weeks later, I found over a thousand dollars which I had "overlooked" the first time.

But the major change in this period of crisis occurred when my mother signed, though with some hesitation, the agreement to give me power of attorney before her first operation. I now came into a position of administrative control and in many ways primary responsibility for my mother's life. Had I let my aunt continue in, or strengthen herself in, that position, I believe I would have been unable to operate in the system as I later did. Ironically, I realized that very clearly when I went to the family lawyer to have it drawn up.

My cousin, my aunt's son, had known this lawyer since childhood, and he had drawn up my mother's will as well as everyone else's. When he saw what I was doing he (gratuitously) advised me that I might be taking my mother's self-confidence away by taking the money out of her hands. I replied, and this became my guiding principle, "I do not believe the issue of confidence for the aged is a matter of how one relates to their money, but how one relates to them."

(2) Rehabilitation

As my mother recuperated from her second operation, the question arose of where she should go when she left the hospital. Her mental state was of such confusion that she seemed unable to join in the decision-making process and she kept asking to go home, or to her room (when she was already in it). The doctor said that she should have medical supervision for from one to three months after she left, and it was the opinion of all the staff that she would never be able to live alone again. The nursing home scandal was at its height in the New York newspapers, and the hospital staff, while helpful in suggesting some places, had little actual contact with the places they recommended. On a day that has to rank as one of the most memorable in my life, I visited ten nursing homes and convalescent centers in the suburbs of New York covering a distance of about one hundred fifty miles from dawn to dusk. My two criteria were these: that the place would have an interest in seeing my mother leave upright, and that it would be situated in a place inconvenient for my aunt to visit, who had never learned to drive a car. I finally chose a convalescent center that was part of a large state hospital system where she was allowed to stay a month.

The day of the move turned out to be a metaphor of the whole scene. I decided to drive to New York with my whole family and take her to the rehabilitation center myself, my aunt begging me not to bring her home first. I did, however, having stocked some of her favorite foods for lunch, and almost immediately she began to

become better oriented. Similarly, all along the drive to the rehabilitation center, each road sign enabled us to encounter memories.

Now, seeing there was hope, with each moment I became more
encouraged that I had found a place that would help get her functioning again. Throughout her hospital stay I would on my visits
walk her up and down the halls, up and down long halls the length
of city blocks. Each time I would be stopped by nurses and aides
telling me I had no permission. I had always responded to these
comments with "I will take responsibility," and as this was duly
recorded in the proper log, I would continue walking with my
mother. When we left the hospital that morning, I was again
stopped as we passed the nursing station and told she must leave in
a wheelchair.

We arrived at the rehabilitation center at noon and walked in
together, my children carrying her things. A phone call was made to
the proper floor, but my spirits sagged as two nurses arrived to take
her, pushing a wheelchair which they insisted she use. It was during
this period that I learned a lesson which would prove to be invaluable later on. It has to do with anxiety and competence, the anxiety
of many professionals and the competence of those they are helping.
There is an inverse ratio between them.

While my mother was at the rehabilitation center, this ratio
manifested itself in two encounters with the head nurse of my
mother's section. On my first visit, after having tried to establish a
good relationship with her, I mentioned my surprise that they were
still making her use a wheelchair. I was told that she had to because
she was very disoriented. Next I tried to explain how much more
confused she had been previously, but that even then she could
walk. I was told that I don't understand her condition. For example,
I was informed she is told always to put the brake on before she sits
down, and she always forgets. To this I said gently, "Well, you know,
while she appears to be a sweet, quick-to-please lady, sometimes she
gets quite rebellious and maybe she's just fighting the idea of always
having to be in a chair." That did it. I was immediately diagnosed:
"Why, Rabbi, do you insist on denying her condition?"

On a second visit the head nurse was not around. It was
lunchtime and I wanted to take my mother off the ward to give her

a change, down to the coffee shop, as I had been allowed to do on the first visit. Actually I could find no nurses at all. Since patients were generally allowed to go about and no one seemed to have objections the first time, I told some aides who were distributing lunch trays so that when someone came to the nursing station they would be informed of my mother's whereabouts. Ten minutes later an anxious phone call to the coffee shop asked to know where my mother was, five minutes after that someone burst in the door looking for Mrs. Friedman, and shortly thereafter the head nurse called me directly at the coffee shop and told me I had overstepped my bounds. The following day the coffee shop was made off-limits to visitors and patients, and a few days later I was informed that they could do nothing more for my mother there and needed her bed.

While I am not generally one to shirk a struggle, it seemed to me that in fighting here I ran the risk of a spin-off that would ricochet to my mother's detriment. I therefore decided on a different approach from here on. First, even though I had done a lot of research myself on the matter of attendants who could live with my mother when she returned home, and I only needed a few bits of additional information to make plans for my next step, I approached those who counseled in such situations with total helplessness and ignorance. I soon found myself struggling to get away from all their overwhelming efforts to help.

But nothing better illustrated the inverse ratio of competence and professional anxiety than what happened three days later. I was supposed to call the social worker assigned to my mother and let her know when I was coming to take my mother out, but she was not in her office. I therefore left a message that everything was working out well and would call her back. Three hours later, a message appeared on my phone answering device in clipped, officious tones, telling me that she was the one I had called, and how I must understand that she is not always at her desk, and to please contact her immediately at the following numbers. I had accidentally done it again! Not only that, but she has probably "heard" about me from the head nurse. So I decided to take an unusual tack. I called the woman back and, mustering up all the anxiety I could put into my voice, I said, with rapid speech and heavy breathing, "Ms. . . . ? This is Rabbi Friedman. What's the matter? Is my mother all right? Did something happen? Your message scared me."

Her response was more than I could have hoped for. She immediately "calmed me down," told me everything I needed to know, and became my mother's sworn advocate—even to the point where, several weeks later when a financial complication arose with the bureaucracy, I made another "helpless" call to her and the problem was solved within a week.

Two or three other incidents occurred during this rehabilitation period that are worthy of note because of their help during the final stretch. First, one day I forgot three things while visiting my mother: where I had parked my rental car, the way to the men's room, and whether I had left my coat in my mother's room or in my car. It suddenly occurred to me that if my mother had done any of those things, we would have attributed it to her condition! Second, I learned that the best way to cut through my mother's obstreperousness, pouting, and denial of her real situation in order to force her to make decisions was to give her choices. For example, on the matter of a home attendant she was balking. She had lived alone for twenty years—why did she have to share her small apartment with someone else? She didn't need anyone. Would she have to sleep in the same room? Would she be black or white? When all efforts failed to prove both that she needed someone and would have to take anyone we got, I began to tell her that those were not the choices. Her choice was not, live in her apartment alone or with someone else, or have someone who was black or white. No, her choice was, would she go back to her apartment or to a nursing home? Indeed, I even started encouraging her to go for the latter because a nursing home would be easier on all of us. From that point on she made no more fuss about a home attendant, and as I shall shortly describe, the sixty-year-old black grandmother who arrived within weeks became a blood relative.

On the day I brought my mother home I also decided to try to rework one of the other cutoffs, that between me and my aunt's son and his wife. I therefore called them the day before and said I would like to throw a coming home party for my mother and take them all out to dinner. My cousin, of course, had bought his mother's perception of things and said that while he would like to go, it was ridiculous to think my mother would be able. It would be too difficult a strain after the trip home (twenty-five miles!) and her relocation. So we left it that I would call again after my mother came home.

Fifteen minutes after my mother came home, my aunt, who had only gotten to visit her once, had made an appointment for her in a beauty parlor. So I called my cousin and said I didn't know about him, but the rest of us would be going to dinner. They came. Looking for some innocuous topic of conversation that would help us to reconnect but not touch some sore point by accident, I hit upon the sweetness of New York City water. For the moment, the family was reunited again as it had not been in years, at least since before my mother had begun deteriorating. But rough seas lay ahead.

(3) Enter Olive

I found Olive through a first cousin of my father's. This was quite ironic, for my mother had never encouraged me to get close to my father's "communist" cousins, but over the years I had fought to get myself past her perceptions of his family. One of them, with whom I had frequent contact and who had laid out my father's entire genealogy for me, worked for the garment unions for years.

Knowing how jealously the unions took care of their own, I figured she would tell me how to find a home attendant. As it happened she knew someone personally who had worked with a terminal cancer patient living on her floor. Poor Olive—moving from a box-like apartment in a walkup where she cared for the last days of a physically degenerating male body, to a lovely, well-lit, and roomy apartment where she would take care of an ambulatory, if somewhat confused, female, she probably thought she was moving from a dungeon to a castle. But the palace would in many ways turn out to be a prison. I calculate that it took six, maybe ten hours from the time Olive moved into my mother's apartment till the moment when the triangle between Olive, my mother, and my aunt became immovably fixed.

By that evening my aunt was already telling me now how "tricky" she was—good, mind you, but "you have to watch her."

My mother, for her part, had only nice things to say about her, while Olive set up a pattern in which she talked only nicely about my mother, and negatively about "the spy down the hall."

Remembering from the hospital days with the social worker that it was easier to deal with a triangle to which I was not integral rather than one in which I was a primary ingredient, I felt great relief. But I also set about trying to see what the best way was of dealing with it. At first I used to pass on a lot of the information each gave me about the other. Later I decided that if I could keep most of the backbiting to myself and not believe what I was being told, I did more to calm the anxiety in the system. (Though some remarks were just too good to keep quiet.) Whatever the individual instance, in general I found I was in a position of managing information that would make any president envious. The question was which channel to keep open at any given time.

I also realized that the conflict between my aunt and Olive usually took pressure off my mother, unless she got caught up in it. On the other hand, I saw quickly that it was quite to my innocent mother's advantage to keep her two "parents" fighting about her.

I had, of course, thought that with someone less tied-in to my mother taking care of her, there would be less pampering and more objectivity about my mother's seductive helplessness. One of the first things I did after this period began, therefore, was to ask my mother to bake me a cheesecake. She was famous for them among all who knew her, and I thought this would be an excellent way to start her functioning again, even though she was not "allowed" to cook. So I explained to Olive which ingredients she would need and how, if she stood beside her, there would be nothing to fear. On my following trip to New York my mother surprised me with the cake. Remembering the taste from my childhood I rushed to eat a piece. Somehow, it was different, though the consistency and appearance were the same. But what did it matter—she could make more, and the old way would come back. After all, she had not made one in a decade. As I soon learned, however, she had not made this one either. My aunt had bought the ingredients, not Olive, and together *they* had baked the cake—under, they assured me, my mother's supervision.

While my mother had been at the rehabilitation center, it was difficult to keep up the process which I had begun when she was in the hospital of having her friends and relatives stay in contact. I now renewed this effort. After all, she had two older remarried brothers living on the island, with cousins and nephews also. I also started a correspondence with a childhood friend of hers living in California who had stayed in touch with my mother over the years, and I made some efforts at involving the Canadian group. The ice had thawed somewhat there, though I could see my cousin was still not quite ready to have me visit. In addition, he was having problems with his own mother, who was only a few years younger than mine. A once proud, sophisticated, elegant woman, she had become a recluse since her husband died and, I understood from my cousin's intimations, oblivious to the appearance of her apartment or herself. She always related well over the phone, however, so I tried to get her to contact my mother more often.

All these efforts bore little fruit, however, first because my mother turned everyone off when they called her with silence, complaints, or confusion, and second, because she never called back. Worse, they all began to call her sister to find out my mother's condition.

One other event of significance should be mentioned from this period, primarily because it serves as a benchmark in my dealing with my aunt's anxiety. Having taken over complete control of my mother's funds, I was the one paying Olive. It was easier to do this by transferring the funds to my own bank. My aunt, however, went at me weekly about the matter. What if something happened to me? "Well, my wife isn't going to run off with it, you know." "But the money should be kept in the hands of a member of the family," she pressed on. At first, I tried to put her off by pointing out that she would certainly have considered her own spouse a member of the family, but I quickly saw that this did not work. In addition, I saw that I was avoiding her in general in order not to deal with her constant harassment over this issue, and I did not like that. I decided therefore, once and for all, that I would no longer be intimidated by her anxiety.

First I tried a playful direction—I would approach her as she approached others, with a sense of injury. I went in and told her how hurt I was that she did not consider my wife a member of the family and that I did not know how long it would take me to get over it. To my stunned surprise she snapped, "Oh, that's nonsense!"

When I got back home I wrote her a short letter. One of her other major complaints to me throughout this period had been the irresponsibility of her two older married brothers, George and Lou, who never came to visit my mother or call her (which was not true), and who had always been shiftless all their lives (also untrue).

The letter went as follows:

Dear Aunt Rose,

I have been giving more thought to your insistence that I make someone in the family the protector of my mother's money. While I am still deeply hurt that you do not consider my wife to be a member of the family, I have decided to follow up on your suggestion. I am contacting George and Lou to ask them if they would be willing to take over the administration of the funds in case anything happens to me. I am sure you will like this idea doubly since it will also have the advantage of sticking them with some responsibility at last, and relieving you of one more burden.

The whole issue disappeared.

Around about this time I realized a second change in my professional functioning. A key officer of the small congregation I served as rabbi went into a period of emotional collapse. It occurred in the middle of an extremely important year for the congregation's survival when stable, solid leadership was crucial. As part of the renaissance of this group, I had been trying to learn how to lead effectively without making the group overly dependent on me. With what, in retrospect, seemed exceptional cool, I contacted several people privately, told them what had to be done, and a meeting of the Board of Trustees was called. Since there was no constitutional provision for replacing an individual and even naming an interim one without the officer herself resigning, everyone was in a quandary. What made matters worse was that the officer had not totally left the scene, but was making periodic and random efforts at "leadership." It was an intolerable position for anyone who would fill her place.

At the meeting, several of the members who were social workers kept worrying aloud that to replace her, even if it was only until she said she was ready to come back, would undercut her confidence in herself at a time when she most needed it. Clearly this worry was going to prevent effective action. Therefore I said, in a manner in which I am not accustomed to speaking, "I believe the first responsibility of this Board of Trustees this evening is to the congregation." Everything went smoothly from there; a new officer was installed, the other notified, and the congregation continued its renaissance without a hitch. The following year, when the former officer "got her confidence," she returned as a fully functioning member of the congregation and even occupied a contributing position on the board.

(4) The Homestretch

My mother's functioning generally improved from the time in February when she left the rehabilitation center till about the summer. She even flew down to Washington with Olive for Passover. She experienced no more fainting spells, though maybe once or twice slipping off into sleep. (During the month at the rehabilitation center, by the way, when she was away from her sister, no episodes at all were reported.)

Somewhere during the summer, however, she reverted to a more childish posture. It seemed to begin after a visit to New York with my four-year-old son. I had left him with her at a table in a restaurant and gone to make a call. He got up to come after me; she got up to chase after him, and she fell, producing a bump on her head literally the size of an orange. There appeared to be no lasting damage, however, and she was better within a week. But shortly after that I began to notice more regression on her part and a higher level of anxiety on her sister's, with Olive agreeing more and more with my aunt's perception of things. And the next time my mother flew down with Olive in September she seemed much more out of it, wanting to call her sister every hour.

After this visit of ten days, in which my mother at times seemed out and out psychotic, I decided to make one more major effort to loosen things up in New York. The doctor had told me that it was all right to leave my mother alone from time to time, but my mother's watchdogs would not do this. Even when Olive went down to do the laundry, it was only after she had deposited my mother with her sister. I therefore got a note from the doctor saying that pampering was not good for my mother and that it would definitely be worth the risk to give her some space once in a while.

Armed with this note, I prepared to make a trip to New York and insist that this be tried. Still wondering what had increased the anxiety in the system, I made a call to my aunt's son. Everything seemed to be going remarkably well for his two children in graduate school, as well as for himself and his wife, in fact, never better. On the other hand, he proceeded to lecture me about my mother's condition. "Listen," he said, "I know about these things (he's a CPA). It's not easy for me to say this, but your mother is manifesting all the classic symptoms of psychosis. She was forgetful, often confused, and from time to time would have moments of frenetic busyness as she emptied drawers and rearranged them." And then, with all the wisdom one only-child cousin thirteen years older than the other could muster, "Eddie, you should really take her to a psychiatrist."

The natural urge, of course, was to remind him what I did for a living. I decided instead to play along with it since I was still looking for something, not realizing I already had it. First I asked him when he had last seen my mother, and he haltingly said, "Not for several months." So I responded, "Listen, you know the new idea in psychiatry is that instead of sending the patient, the members of the family who have the most strength should go so that they can learn how to pull the patient up. Maybe your mother is the one who should go."

Another issue disappeared.

The next evening, in front of my mother's oldest brother and his wife (she had herself just returned from a short stay at a psychiatric institution), I told my aunt and Olive what I wanted. My aunt totally blew up. I had seen her anxious before, but never so scared.

I was hoping to use the doctor's note only for my own sense of confidence, but I now produced it as evidence of my position. Olive objected, "She's not ready yet." When I pressed further, my aunt told me I was crazy. When I said I was paying for my mother's help and would decide how she should be helped, she said, "With whose money?" She threatened to get a lawyer. Flabbergasted, but surprisingly in control, I told her sternly that if she did that, I would have her committed.

Through all of this, which took place right in front her, she was like a spectator. And then, as usual, she responded to my efforts on her part by saying that her sister was only trying to help her. I now fed back what her son had told me the night before: that she needed a psychiatrist, wanting to know where he came off suggesting something like that, and what was my aunt telling him about my mother? She walked out, but returned half an hour later to see how my mother was doing.

When I returned to Washington, I wrote my cousin that as appreciative as I was about his mother's helpfulness, it wasn't. (He had recently described his mother as the kind of person who, if she didn't worry about something, would worry about the fact that she didn't have something to worry about.) I also reminded him that it was not my mother who had never learned to drive a car, had never been in a plane, and was afraid of boats, and that as far as psychosis went, I thought its hallmark was becoming inextricably involved in someone else's relationship. I ended by saying that I was going to do whatever I thought necessary to keep my mother going, and that if his mother got in the way, that would have to be her responsibility.

When I got to New York two weeks later, I met my aunt in the street. She told me her son had left on a vacation for Florida. He had begged her to go with him but she just couldn't. Standing there in the cold, New York winter sunlight, my aunt suddenly seemed very small and frail. That was the last time I made a big head-on effort. For the next six months I just kept working with the basic triangle of my mother, her sister, and Olive. My mother's money had run out, but luckily in New York City Medicaid will pay for an at-home attendant. From time to time things became more intense, as when my mother would faint, cut her head, and have to be rushed to "The Annex" on the next block.

I tried different methods of dealing with my mother on the phone, and tried to observe the results from different patterns of calls, say, the number of times a week I phoned as compared to which of the three ladies I spoke to. During this period my aunt and I got closer than we had been since third grade—when she had drilled me in my multiplication tables when, out of school for six weeks with whooping cough, we sat along the Hudson River looking at flashcards.

Between Two Cemeteries

This final essay recalls a visit to family graves some time after Friedman's bypass surgery and recovery.

I had not visited my parents' grave in several years. It had been my custom to go yearly, but since my bypass operation the anxiety of that close call had lessened my desire to be with them again so quickly. I also decided to visit my grandparents' grave, my mother's parents. They were buried more than forty miles away, across the rivers, but I had my own car this trip, I was alone, I had time, and with today's highways it would be an easy detour. I had not been to their grave in more than thirty years. In fact, I doubt anyone had, off the beaten track as it was now, somewhere between old neighborhoods of long-forgotten dates and friends, surrounded by a baseball stadium built for a team not then in existence and the grounds of the 1964 World's Fair, disappeared forever except for those iron monuments of the world left as playgrounds for grandchildren and urinals for pets.[10] Unlike my parents, who had the foresight to be buried within five minutes of the Garden State Parkway and twenty minutes from "the Bridge," my grandparents had gotten themselves

---

10. The 1964–65 World's Fair was held in Flushing Meadows Corona Park in the Borough of Queens. Here Friedman may be referring to the site of the Unisphere, a famous twelve-foot-high stainless-steel sculpture of the earth.

stuck in a wide enclave of undulating freeways that gave their vicin-
ity visibility but little access. Surely that would never be the fate of
my parents' lovely piece of land in Paramus.

I arrived about eleven o'clock. One could see the entire cemetery,
every single rectangular white stone, at a glance. The usual Sunday
rush hour had begun. Cars (mostly big cars) parked every which
way, and then long chains of funeral processions connecting up, re-
ceiving directions, and snaking their way in and out of maneuvers
among the "blocks." Everything was so simple, so proper, so orderly.
Stones, all the same size and shape and color and girth, all laid out
as if some computer had created the grid and was still in charge,
monitoring, in the name of perpetuity, the status quo. Even a blade
of grass that crossed a boundary would have been told to go back.

I followed the familiar perpendicular pathways without difficulty to the grave and pulled alongside. As I slowly passed the other
mourners in my blue and silver Zephyr, I sensed the "loudness" of
my disturbing presence. Not only that, there was my disconcerting
and foreign Maryland license. I remember once as a kid, I think I
was nine, we New Yorkers had gone out on a Sunday to visit Aunt
Mary's grave after she died. All anyone talked about on the way back
was the yellow convertible from "way down South" in Virginia:
"Hey, you should have seen the 'Z' from Maryland at the unveiling!"

Cars passed slowly behind me as I stood looking down on my
parents' grave. One single man, alone with a sports car, crying. My
parents used to call it their "eight-room house in the country." They
had been cliff dwellers their entire lives. Me, too, until I bought my
modern townhouse in the Bethesda woods where I have lived ever
since, and watched my kids and my cats and my marriage grow old.
Now I also have an eight-room house, at the beach! My folks got the
whole dwelling for half the cost of a single room today. Why eight
plots with an only child? They figured geometrically: there'd be
room for me and my wife and my kids and their wives. No one
imagined any other kind of separation. Finally, they sold off two
plots to my mother's sister, who's still going strong. At least they
have the company of her husband, their brother-in-law, in the
meantime. I offered the remaining two to their son, my cousin. He
lives in walking distance, but he's going with his wife's folks.

There was a time when I thought cemeteries were a waste of land. After all, some day we'll run out, won't we? Or maybe by then we'll all be on another planet, and Sundays will still be for visiting Earth. But today I realize there is nothing like it for remaining in touch. People say, "I carry my memories with me." Nonsense. You may carry them with you, but what's going to prompt you to remember? Not some piece of pottery with everyday familiarity. It's more than that; it's a reminder of our own earthliness. It's even more than that; it's a reminder of our extension in time. Maybe that's what "extended" families are about. It's the inscriptions, the dates, the relationships, and the recognition that there are other mourners, too.

I always cry; that's why I like to go alone. I cry for my childhood which went so fast, and for the warmth I never had again, and for the love, if poorly expressed, and for the failed opportunities of comradeship which, in spite of my awareness today, I see my own children losing with me. But it helps me remind me that I'm me: somehow, the memories have less ghostly power when they are remembered in the presence of the Reminders. And I always leave more loving and more committed to my own. And sometimes, I get a new thought, like the time when I found myself thanking my father for the talents and abilities he gave me rather than cursing him for the personality problems I "inherited." Or the moment when I heard a voice say, "Live your life, not mine," or that instant of recognition that my parents were at least united again after twenty-five years and I was indeed free to be me. This time a double message, inspired by the anxiety of my rearranged inner tubing—"Take all the time you need to finish your work," and then as I was leaving, "but don't take too long."

I headed for the bridge. When I was a kid, I remember my mother telling me of slow, sweaty Sunday journeys like this when she was a kid to see the immigrant relatives, but they were to living relatives. To grandmother's house I go. It is forty miles but it's only forty minutes, provided I make it to the right interchanges and take the right bridge and use the right turnoffs. I did, but I forgot—there is still an immigrant generation of living relatives for other

New Yorkers to visit on such Sundays. The traffic snarls double my time.

I don't think I had visited my grandmother's grave since her death. I was about seventeen then. Maybe I was at her unveiling, but in those days I probably didn't notice, for my head was more filled with Dedalus than Moses.[11] Me, trying to create in "the smithy of my soul, the uncreated consciousness of my race," to forge together, somehow, Beethoven and Brubeck, Thornton Wilder and John Coltrane, but above all Mt. Sinai and the castle at Howarth. Did I not, as the student rabbi, travel to Dublin less to read the progressives in prayer than to see "The Dubliners," and to walk in Leopold Bloom's footsteps rather than to preach to his relatives?

But I had gone to this gravesite many times with my grandmother, my folks, and her still-going-strong daughter to visit her husband, my grandfather, who was dying of leukemia all during my mother's pregnancy, and who saw the newborn once, I think, and who died when I was seven months old. It was he whom I replaced in all the family triangles, since my newly widowed grandmother then came to live with us and taught me about the old country—how her mother died when she was born, and how she left Warsaw to come here at seventeen, and who was the only babysitter I ever knew. And whom I shall thank till my dying breath for her foresight, which saved me from the camps and the chimneys and the smell of Zyklon B. I paid my dues as well as any survivor can, traveling alone to Warsaw in 1956 and standing there on that wide, weed-sprouting stretch of shack-strewn land that was once the final ghetto. I somehow made sense of the Polish train tables to go, once again alone, to the town of Auschwitz to see the museum mounds of hair and brushes and hats, and walk a mile to those showers whose floors only became wet when it rained, and touch the oven door, left open.

How I hated going to the cemetery! It was always hot (we never went in the winter) and I had no one to play with. There was always anxiety about finding the right block number, the right lodge gate,

---

11. Stephen Dedalus, the protagonist of James Joyce's novel *A Portrait of the Artist as a Young Man*. Other references are to the favorite writers and composers of Friedman's adolescence.

the right grave row, and all the traffic jams in the narrow roads. And the little old bearded men who wanted to say prayers—aggressive little old men with suction shoes like flies, who clung on the running boards and could not be shooed away but for twenty-five cents and a psalm. There was a bench, a little round bench with a tall tree in the middle. I always wanted to sit there because the sun made me tired, but I was afraid of the bees that always hovered nearby. I suddenly remembered that for the first time in thirty years.

This time I had to drive completely around the cemetery, twice, before I found the entrance. I found two of those little men. They used to know all the directions inside; now they know the way around outside. "Double back through service roads and underpasses," they explained as I poured quarters into their palms. I wondered, "Will the cemetery even let cars in anymore, and will they have a record of the grave? How long will the line be to get the information?" I was hungry and tired.

As I drove through the main gate in my Japanese time machine, I began to remember more. It was a big place, much bigger than my parents'. It was hilly, and the stones—I had forgotten the stones, all different sizes, different shapes, different colors, some with polished granite balls on top, all with beautiful engraving, some with pictures of people the way they dressed more than a hundred years ago. Their height, combined with the hilly terrain, meant there was no way to see more than a fraction of the place. But the hills and the tall trees (my parents' suburban neighborhood had no trees) and the stones themselves created privacy and seclusion. It was majestic. I think I used to be scared of these stones. But I am more than six feet tall now. They are still bigger.

At the office they found the gravesite very fast, considering there were six people buried there with the exact same first and last name. Luckily I knew the date of her death. How could I forget that? It was the same as the date of my daughter's birth (I had even given her an extremely similar name, never imagining a link). I found the site easily enough. The atmosphere reminded me of Israel; just an association? The Hebrew? The sun? The dirt roads? I found her block, the Zephyr incongruent again, not because of the other cars this time, but because of the stones. Block 11 was subdivided into twelve

entrances, each with a little gate for the "lodge." Then I tried to find
the right row. But the little round bench, that would tell me, and the
tree. The right spot had really been smack in front of my car but I
walked the wrong way, circled the block in the wrong direction.
Thus, by the time I found it, I had stumbled and searched among
their contemporaries for almost fifteen minutes. Several times the
last name was correct but something else wasn't, and the lodge
names were all so similar. And then, suddenly, the right lodge,
shalem, "peace," immediately in front of the car. It would be down,
and to the left, I knew that. There, the bench, the round bench, but
it had only a little bush growing in the middle, after thirty years! The
tree I knew had evidently died among these living souls, and they
simply put a bush in.

Unlike my parents' neighborhood, I could not stand in a con-
venient way and look down, but had to squiggle and squirm to get
close among the rows. I could not avoid stepping on the graves of
others. But there it was. And the stones made you look up! The last
time I came I barely could have read the Hebrew; at least I would
not have known what it meant. Now, three decades later, and a rabbi
and a family therapist, for the first time in my life I knew my grandfather's first name, Avigdor. Incredibly, I had once used that very
name in a short story thinking it was biblical in origin, but I was unable to find it in any concordance when I tried to understand its
hidden significance. Was this the significance? Of course, Victor,
Avigdor, my two cousins are named Victor. It was he, Avigdor,
whom I replace in my grandmother's affections—not, as I have long
assumed, her husband whose untimely death my overdue birth preceded. Not her husband, but her father.

I remember now the stories of his learning, his erudition.
Grandpa was just a tailor, a sweet man, but Avigdor, he was a
scholar. That also explains my uncanny desire to know my cousins
once removed. If it had been Grandpa, then the strange closeness I
felt to my family would have ended with my first cousins, but
through Avigdor I am linked to his other children also—my great-
aunt and my great-uncle. That link cannot be through their brother-
in-law—it must be through their father! Avigdor, who lost his
beloved wife after bearing their sister, my grandmother, whom they

brought with them here to America to get away, not from the pogroms, but from his second wife, their stepmother. Avigdor the second time had married a shrew! I heard that also years ago. My God, it's more than that, for my grandmother would have replaced that mother she never knew in his affections. It made her special, and she passed on the specialness as she reciprocated, replacing him with me. Poor Grandpa, he was bypassed.

But I did not get the feeling I expected. Unlike my visit to my parents' grave, these were two strangers with whom I could not "carry on a conversation." They did not answer, so I left them in peace, at last, and started back to town.

And then it hit me. I was all alone. Where was the tumult and turmoil of yesteryear? There were no traffic jams, no one to jump on running boards, no one wailing or rending their clothes, no funeral processions forming, and this place ten times the size of the other. Of course—how could there be? The people who used to visit here are now themselves being visited over there, on the other side of the rivers, across the Hudson, where I just came from. There are not too many left of my generation to come here and visit.

And when the bonus runs out, beyond what river will I be visited? Surely the intergenerational chain will not receive additional links. It was a one-generation phenomenon to visit and be visited. Surely fifty years from now no one will come from California or the Sunbelt to look down or up. Even less is the possibility that if they do, others will be there to be disconcerted by the loud presence of such a one who fords the Potomac.